DINER

PHOENICIA DINER

Gizelle's Bucket List

My Life with a Very Large Dog

Lauren Fern Watt

SIMON & SCHUSTER

New York London Toronto Sydney New Delhi

Simon & Schuster
1230 Avenue of the Americas
New York, NY 10020

First Simon & Schuster hardcover edition March 2017

SIMON & SCHUSTER and colophon are registered trademarks of Simon & Schuster, Inc.

The names and characteristics of some individuals in this book have been changed.

For information about special discounts for bulk purchases, please contact Simon & Schuster Special Sales at 1-866-506-1949 or business@simonandschuster.com.

The Simon & Schuster Speakers Bureau can bring authors to your live event. For more information or to book an event, contact the Simon & Schuster Speakers Bureau at 1-866-248-3049 or visit our website at www.simonspeakers.com.

Manufactured in the United States of America

1   3   5   7   9   10   8   6   4   2

Library of Congress Cataloging-in-Publication Data

Names: Watt, Lauren Fern, author.
Title: Gizelle's bucket list : my life with a very large dog / Lauren Fern Watt.
Description: New York: Simon & Schuster, 2017.
Identifiers: LCCN 2016033521 | ISBN 9781501123658 (hardcover) | ISBN 9781501123665 (pbk.)
Subjects: LCSH: Mastiff—New York (State)—New York. | Watt, Lauren Fern. | Human-animal relationships.
Classification: LCC SF429.M56 W38 2017 | DDC 636.70092/9—dc23
LC record available at https://lccn.loc.gov/2016033521

ISBN 978-1-5011-2365-8
ISBN 978-1-5011-2367-2 (ebook)

To my dad for teaching me to "hang in there"

Contents

Author's Note

While writing this book, I referenced personal journals, spoke with family and friends who appear in the story, and reflected on my memories of growing up with my very large dog, Gizelle. The book spans around seven years of my life, so by necessity events essential to this narrative were chosen, and other events were left out. Some names and identifying characteristics of individuals in this book have been changed.

Prologue

The alarm rang from my phone and I reached over to hit snooze. I snuggled my head back into the pillow and it beeped again. With one eye barely open, I thumbed at the screen. "Shit! Shit! Shit!" I jumped out of bed, grabbed a running shirt from the mountain of clothes, threw on my Asics, and bolted out the door.

I ran to the Astor Place subway, took the train up to Central Park, and sprinted to the registration tent. Out of breath upon arrival, I was met by a woman with long red fingernails and a raised eyebrow. "Hon, you are twenty minutes late."

"But this is one of my qualifying runs for the New York City Marathon." I pleaded. "I only have to *complete* this race. Please, *please* just let me run." She placed her hands over the plastic bin of bibs and pinched her lips together. "That race is gone."

Backing out of the tent, tears filled my eyes. *Don't cry. Don't cry. Don't cry. Not here, Lauren. Not in Central Park.* But there was no stopping it. Once I blinked, the tears came flooding.

Head down, I wandered across the park to Bethesda Fountain, the spot where Gizelle and I liked to watch the rowboats in the pond. She'd been having trouble with her back left leg. The stairs of my walk-up apartment building were too much, so two friends with a one-story house in Maine had offered to babysit for a few weeks. This made it possible for me to return to the city and carry on with work, but it was lonely in the city without Gizelle. Caitlin and John said she was doing well and staying off her paws. She was taking her medicine with ease. She would come back to New York as soon as she was well . . . at least that's what I hoped. But then again I wasn't so sure. Every time I thought about her limp, this horrible fear came over me.

I took a deep breath and wiped my face with my shirt. *Okay, Lauren. Just because you missed one race doesn't mean you can't have a race of your own instead. You can still run your miles.* I shook off the tears and started running. I ran up the stairs and through the elm trees, imagining Gizelle's giant paws tapping at my side like they always did before she'd developed that stupid limp. I continued around the duck pond, circled the Alice in Wonderland sculpture, then broke out of the park to Fifth Avenue.

I kept running. The heat from the concrete rose up to my legs. It would have been too hot for Gizelle to run today, but that didn't stop me from still picturing her by my side. When I closed my eyes, I could almost hear her paws tapping next to me. Faster and faster I ran down Fifth Avenue, dodging the crowds of busy Saturday traffic in Manhattan, feeling better with every stride.

I made my way over to Seventh Street, crossed Avenue A and considered running another mile or two to the East

River Promenade, but instead stopped in front of my apartment. I exhaled and dropped my hands to my knees. Exhale. Exhale. Exhale. I took my phone out of my running armband. It was then I noticed the three missed calls. There was voicemail waiting. It was from Caitlin. She said to call right away. It was about Gizelle.

I climbed the stairs to my apartment out of breath. *Maybe Caitlin is calling about her food or her prescriptions?* The vet had called in some of her meds to be filled at the Rite Aid in Kittery. Maybe there was a problem picking it up. My face was flushed from the seven miles, my Asics were still on, and my heart pounded. I opened the door to my apartment and Gizelle's empty dog bed and stared at my phone, trying to work up the courage to just call. *Just call, Lauren. It's fine.*

How quickly Gizelle had come into my life, a summer day in Tennessee six years before. Back when my parents were still together, before I moved to New York City, before I started running. How quickly Gizelle had become my new best friend, but so much more.

I dialed the number.

PART I

Enchanted

1

A Big Puppy

We promised ourselves we were just going to *look*. Mom and I were sitting in the parking lot of CVS on Franklin Road. It was 10 a.m. and humid already in Brentwood, the suburb of Nashville where I grew up. The windshield faced a line of trees and we were facedown in the *The Tennessean* classifieds, shopping in our favorite section. The puppy section.

We had no business browsing in the puppy section that day. Back home we already had two dogs, Yoda and Bertha, not to mention a slew of other critters and this other unsolvable family problem I doubted the new puppy would know how to fix.

"Lab?" I suggested, biting into my everything bagel.

Mom shook her head, mouth full, too. She gave me a thumb up in the air. *Bigger!*

"Coonhound?"

"Ehh." She thought it over. "Isn't a coonhound UT's mascot or something, sweetie?" She was right. The droopy-eared, jowly coonhound was the mascot of the Vols, the football team at the University of Tennessee where I'd be starting as a transfer sophomore in the fall. Would purchasing the mascot be a little too smells-like-team-spirit for the new girl on campus? Having the same thought, our eyes met and we both smiled.

Ever since I'd come home this summer, Mom had developed a new hankering for facetime in the mornings, suggesting a Starbucks/Bruegger's bakery hit-and-run a few times a week: bagels to go and some super-sugary coffee thing. Then we'd park the car in an empty parking lot somewhere just a few miles from a proper kitchen table in our own house, this way we could "talk." Just the two of us.

And in my mother's case, our talks usually consisted of her apologizing and reminding me she was "totally 100 percent fine." Then she would look down at her lap, waiting for my usual: "It's okay. It's fine! I believe you." And then we would move on—even though it wasn't okay, and I wasn't sure what I believed anymore.

My mom was my best friend; of course I wanted to believe her. She wrote me notes in my lunchbox until I graduated high school (sometimes including glitter confetti), told us mermaids were real, bought my little sister, Erisy, and me clothes we didn't need. "Don't tell Daddy," she'd whisper in her soft, high, lilting voice (the same voice she passed on to me), before hurrying us to our rooms with shopping bags. She approached all things as if they were supposed to be fun, and if there wasn't anything exciting about some detail of life, she'd create it.

And on this particular Saturday morning, Mom's face lit up with puppy fever. We were sitting in our parked car. Stopped. But it felt like we were in motion. My Frappucino was sweating in its cup holder, the wheels in Mom's head were spinning, no doubt wondering what she could do to make up for last night. She turned her head and looked at me.

"Know what *I* wanna do today?" She leaned in and smiled. "We need to get another puppy."

She took a sip of her Grande coffee. "I really want to

get you a big dog. We're big-dog girls. You're *such* a big-dog girl, sweetie." I didn't even know what it meant to be a big-dog girl, and I didn't care. I placed my bagel on the dashboard, left the Frappuccino melting, and ran into the CVS to fetch the newspaper.

We spread the classifieds across the front of the car, draping the grayish-white pages over our laps and onto the dashboard.

German shepherd?

Active and sporty, that would be nice. But would a shepherd get along well with our other dogs? We had to consider Yoda and Bertha.

Goldendoodle?

Beautiful dogs, but we were thinking, like, a *big* big dog. Great Pyrenees . . .

Oh! Definitely big, but would that be too much fur?

Boxer?

We knew boxers intimately, had loved and lost two when I was younger.

And just as we were about to call the number on an ad for a husky/lab mix, Mom slammed her finger down onto the newspaper, crinkling it further into her lap.

"ENGLISH MASTIFF PUPPIES!"

There's this saying in the mastiff world, "What the lion is to the cat, the mastiff is to the dog." Mastiffs are powerful, gentle, and known for their loyalty. They also happen to be known as the largest dog breed on earth. One Old English mastiff with the name of Aicama Zorba set the record for world's biggest dog at nearly 350 pounds. That's the size of a small donkey. So it's no wonder ancient Greeks and Romans used the mastiff as a war dog. The mastiffs even fought in the Colosseum, next to the gladiators.

Mom put the phone on speaker as it rang. I was so excited I was practically holding my breath, hoping someone would pick up.

"Hello?" A woman answered. She sounded very Southern. The word "hello" sounded like "yellow."

Mom asked if they had a girl.

Yes.

She asked if they had a brindle.

Yes.

Then Mom asked if we could come look (*look*) at the puppies today.

Yes.

Like, right now?

Yes.

So against all reason and good judgment we hopped on I-65 to look.

Our home had always been something of a zoo. Growing up, my brother, sister, and I had every kind of pet a child's heart could desire: furry ones, feathery ones, slimy ones, ones with shells, even one that went *oink*.

If there is an animal-loving gene, I inherited it from my mother. Apparently, when I was little, I would run to the sidewalk after it rained and rescue worms by putting them back in the soil so they didn't dry up. This may sound extreme, but I had nothing on my mother's history with animals.

When Mom was a girl (she tells me) she ordered crocodiles from a catalog and put them in her father's bathtub.

"Can *we* order crocodiles?" I used to beg.

"No, sweetie. It's actually not very nice to the crocodiles. I didn't know better then."

I don't think it's much of an exaggeration to say my mother had been bringing home animals for over fifty years. Mostly without asking. That's actually how we'd gotten our two dogs, Yoda and Bertha—on a whim, from the newspaper. Yoda was our Chihuahua at the time. My older brother, Tripp, referred to her as the rat. Sure, she was not much bigger than a guinea pig, and only had five teeth, but I loved her. Yoda's principal canine companion was Bertha, our English bulldog, who looked more like a beached elephant seal mixed with a pig. She had a funny pink tail that curled into her bum like a cinnamon roll, so my brother, sister, and I named it the Cinnabum. At some point she got the nickname Fatty, and that nickname never went away. Fatty preferred not to exercise, had the worst table manners, and snored loudly enough to wake the neighbors. Still, on summer evenings over the sound of the cricket wings chirping from the forest of our backyard, I was known to sit and gaze at Bertha, and sing "You Are So Beautiful" to her. Fatty was Dad's favorite.

You know the couple who gets pregnant, believing somehow that having a baby will save their marriage? This may have been Mom's thinking in us getting a third dog that day. *A new dog is a fresh start!* It's starting over.

So here we were again, starting over . . .

Two hours later we turned off the exit in Sparta and drove up a long dirt road to a little white house. There was a deep bark booming from the backyard.

A woman opened the screen door.

"Y'all here for mastiff puppies? You can come 'round this way," she said, pointing around to the back.

We followed her to the rear of the house, that deep bark getting closer. A long string of deep, sharp woofs with pauses between each one.

I started to wonder if this was a good idea after all. I felt a twinge of anger at having been convinced to come on this possibly ridiculous trip. Did Mom really think she could just slap a Band-Aid over her messy slurring drunkenness from last night with a puppy? A puppy is a huge decision. A *family* decision. Shouldn't we talk to Dad about this? A wave of guilt washed over me as I imagined my parents ignoring each other even more because Mom and I had brought home another animal.

We entered the yard and Mom clenched my hand with excitement. The barking grew louder. "Oh, that's just Dozer!" The woman swatted a fly from her face, "Don't mind her barkin'; she's gentle as butter." But this was unlike any bark I'd heard. It was big and loud and ominous, as if she knew we had arrived. My stomach sank. We walked farther until we reached a little pen made of chicken wire.

"There's two boys an' two girls left," the woman told us. Inside the pen was a tangle of four adorable mastiff puppies. Their heads were the size of big grapefruits and their coats were streaked with splotchy black stripes. Underneath the stripes, two were chocolate brown, and the other two were shaded a little lighter, closer to the color of sand. The dark coloring on their faces created the appearance of black masks, and one had a little white patch on her chest. They trotted through the grass with round bellies and thick tails and pawed at each other playfully.

I lifted my legs one by one over the wire, sat in the grass, and tried to relax. Mom joined, legs crossed next to me, and as the puppies climbed all over us, Mom's mouth broke into a huge smile. We pianoed our hands under their bellies and let them chew on our shoelaces. Mom buried her nose into their backs, kissing their heads and telling each one it was the cutest thing she'd ever seen. I took a deep breath. Slowly, I felt myself softening toward my mother. Maybe this adventure wasn't such a terrible idea after all. The grass was dry like hay but sprinkled with yellow dandelions. When I close my eyes and remember that day, I can see them. Yellow dandelions and a brindle puppy. My puppy.

The lady bent over to pick up the puppy, turning it on its back to check for its parts. "Here, this one's a girl," she confirmed, and plopped her in my lap. I held her out in front of me with my hands under her armpits. Her skin was too big for her body so it draped over my fingers, and to me this one was so obviously a girl, I couldn't believe the woman had to check. I stared into her eyes and she stared right back. Her wrinkled black forehead and down-turned eyes gave her a concerned expression, making her look a tiny bit sad, but I knew she wasn't, because her tail was wagging. She was prettier than a Gerbera daisy. The puppy reached out her wrinkly neck and nibbled my nose. She did this gently—delicate and deliberate—so her sharp teeth didn't even hurt.

Mom squeezed my knee. "Lauren. Oh my gosh. We *have* to get this puppy! Isn't she incredible? Do you want her?" She searched my face for a response. Dozer was still barking, and from the corner of my eye I could see her behind a metal gate ten or so yards away. Her head was as big as Darth Vader's, and when she barked, frothy slobber flew from her mouth and globbed on the fence.

I held the puppy's warm body to my face and she licked my cheek. That peculiar smell of puppy breath was enough to unzip me. All I wanted was to say yes.

"Mom, I love her." This was true. But there was a part of me that wanted to say, *Let's think about this.* Still, I knew if we didn't leave with this precious puppy today, I would never see her again. My mother's eyes were lit with desperation. "I *want* you to have her, honey. It would make me so happy to get her for you. *Let* me get her for you."

I didn't really understand my family's dynamics back then, and, frankly, at that point, puppy in lap, who even cared if I was being manipulated? I could have called and asked Dad, but Dad would tell me that impulsive pet buying from the newspaper didn't sound like the best idea.

(Rightly so, please don't buy puppies impulsively like this. Also, please consider adopting.)

The warm puppy nibbled my nose again and licked my eye, and then licked me again on the mouth. So I swallowed my worries back down and shut the door to the part of my brain that was saying *Think of the consequences!*

"*Yes!* Let's get her!"

Mom gave the woman $150 cash, then quickly drove to a gas station ATM to take out another $250, and then wrote a check for $300 (we paid for a lot of impulse purchases in this way). I tossed my new friend over my shoulder, thanked the woman very much, gave one last look over to Dozer, and we drove back to Brentwood, one large family member bigger.

"What should we name her?" Mom asked when we were back in the car.

I wanted her name to be something sweet and girly, not like the tractor name they'd given her mom.

"She's such a little lady, a princess," I said, squeezing her to my face.

"What about Please-Dad-don't-get-rid-of-me?" my mother laughed, reaching her hand over to pet the puppy's ears.

The puppy felt so right in my lap. I looked down at her and couldn't believe this was real. Years later, I'd recognize this look as the way a few of my friends gazed at their shiny engagement rings, like they are about to start their lives, like their adventures were about to begin. That's how I'd felt with the dog in my lap, looking into her marble eyes traced by tiny eyelashes. I felt as though I'd fallen under a spell, enchanted. Wait a minute. *Enchanted.* (I may or may not have watched this Disney musical a million times.)

Giselle.

"Mom! What about Giselle? Like the princess in *Enchanted?*" Giselle had such a fun ring to it, and based on a lovable naive character it seemed a fit for this innocent puppy.

"Yes! That's it. Love that!" Mom cheered. We decided to spell it with a *z* for a little extra spunk.

"Hi, Gizelle, hi, girl!" I cooed, cradling her in my arms like a doll. (A heftier, pug-sized doll with longer legs.) "But what are we telling Dad?" I worried, fondling Gizelle's extra neck skin in my hand. Though I knew when it came to this new puppy, he wouldn't be mad. Dad was the most patient person I knew. So he'd probably end up nodding his head, as if to say, *Of* course *they brought home another animal,* and then he'd end up taking care of said animal like he always did, with a minor silent grudge. But he'd get over it. Still, Mom wanted to come up with something that would smooth Dad over, just in case. Something that would lessen the shock of a new puppy. (The new puppy that just happens to be the biggest breed in the world.) So we came up with a plan.

We pulled up the long driveway to our brick house on the hill. As I headed inside, Dad was in the living room practicing his golf swing in front of the TV. As planned, I greeted him and explained that I rescued a puppy from a place I knew nearby called Noah's Ark Animal Hospital. I told him her adoption was free, and that I was only foster-ing her until they found her another home. I couldn't just leave her there to die! I couldn't believe I had been so lucky to rescue her just in time! What. A. Miracle!

Dad studied me with a puzzled look, club still in hand. Usually, Dad would hand me the nine iron and say, "C'mon, let's see that backswing of yours, Fernie. It's really looking great this year!" But he didn't do that. Not today. Instead, he stared down at the size of the huge paws of the puppy cradled in my arms as I worked to pose Gizelle so her ador-able head and heart-melting eyes were working for maxi-mum effect. He looked at me again. He didn't channel an angry, "No. We have two dogs and a fish and Mom brings home too many pets. Take her back where she came from at once!" like a lot of my friends' parents would say, and he didn't go the whole, "Yes, let's foster her until she gets a fur-ever home! Way to give back, Fernie!" route. He just said, "Okay," drawing out the "ay" sound at the end, almost like he was asking a question. And when he squinted his eyes and opened his mouth to say something else, I jumped in. "We aren't keeping her for long!" Once I started lying to Dad, I couldn't stop. For a brief second, I could hear a faint voice inside whispering, *Psst! Stop!* But I told that girl to shut up, that we are meant to have this puppy, and that I will do everything I can to make it work.

2

Sisterhood

Lauren with Yoda, Bertha, and Gizelle

One month later, Gizelle and I were lying on the cold kitchen floor facing each other, me with one arm over her body, she with all four paws tucked into my belly. Yoda glared at us from a kitchen chair. Bertha lumbered in snorting around for crumbs. Gizelle's eyelids began to flicker into an afternoon dream and I was about to close mine, too, when—

"How big's this dog gonna get?" Dad's voice made me jump. "Is it me or is she growing kinda fast?" He looked down as he took a wide step over Gizelle and me.

I stood up to examine her. She was about fifty pounds and if I was going to be honest, she looked more like a full-grown lab than a three-and-a-half-month-old puppy. "I bet not that big, Dad. She's still easy to carry." Bending over to pick her up and show off Gizelle's slenderness, I wrapped my arms around her silky tummy and attempted to lift her in front of my father, but for a moment she didn't budge. I squatted and tried lifting from my legs, but Gizelle was like lifting an office water jug. I planted my feet as widely as I could, engaged my core, gripped my toes to the floor, *three, two, one, heave!* I let out a short, pathetic grunt as I got her off the ground. *Oof.* Her front paws dangled out in front of me, and I had to thrust my pelvis forward to keep my balance. But I was holding her. I could hold her. Dad squinted his eyes at us.

"So how long we keeping the puppy?"

"Oh, not much longer."

I had to strain to get the words out.

Of course, "not much longer" in my dictionary meant

forever and ever. And my dumb teenage self actually thought . . . *what?* That Dad would fall in love with the "foster" puppy, agree to keep her, and never ask another question again? I was living in denial. I was very good at living in denial.

When we first brought Gizelle home, I was convinced our new pet was a sign my mother was sorry, and that this time she would take responsibility, work on a recovery program, and get sober. For a few days she was more like the mom I remembered as a child—first up in the morning, feeding the dogs, burning toast, and arranging fruit in the shape of smiley faces. She was out in the yard with me doing "puppy poopie pickup," as she called it, laughing and joking as she helped pick up the smelly dog poo.

But as the novelty of the new puppy wore off and the responsibility of the new family member set in, she started sleeping in again. Late. And sometimes she went to bed early—like sun-is-still-up early. "I wasn't feeling well. Didn't sleep well last night, girls. The Sudafed really messed with me!" She was always making excuses, and with Mom, it was difficult to filter out what was true and what wasn't.

Then one afternoon I found her passed out on our big blue denim couch, cheek smooshed into the pillow, her mouth agape, arm dangling from the couch, fingertips brushing the floor—almost like she'd fallen into this position. Yoda was sleeping, too, snuggled up against Mom's chest and cradled in one arm. The house phone rang. A muffled ring, coming from underneath Mom and Yoda. Mom's cheek didn't leave the pillow, but her eyelids flickered.

Should I wake her? Force her to pull herself together before Erisy and Dad got home? Erisy hated seeing Mom passed out. But if I woke her, I would then have to deal with her. The phone rang again.

Mom began to move. She reached in slow motion to answer it, but instead grabbed Yoda around the midsection, nuzzling her cheek into the Chihuahua's belly.

Grrrrr, Yoda growled. (You did not disturb Yoda mid-slumber.)

"Hulloooh?" Mom garbled.

Yoda growled again, louder this time.

Mom continued murmuring into our angry Chihuahua's belly until the ringing came to a stop. Then she released her grip on our sweet dog and Yoda scurried back into the warm crevice between Mom and the couch.

I let out a short frustrated exhale and stood for a moment, unable to decide if I should laugh or cry. "Mom!" I finally called out, shaking her. Nothing. She was back asleep. So, I did what most teenagers would do: I called my older brother, named the incident "Yoda-phone," and we carried on with summer, trying to pretend we didn't care.

Carrying on with summer was easier to do with a new puppy around. Maybe I knew what Mom meant when she'd said I was a big-dog girl, because Gizelle and I had a thing from the start. When I got home, Gizelle would follow me from the living room to my bedroom, then back down the stairs and even into the bathroom, where she sat, at my toes, as though I needed her support. I learned quickly that I couldn't step backward without looking. She loved resting her muzzle on my knee, lap, foot, hand. And if she couldn't reach her whiskered snout to some part of me, she resorted to the next closest thing—resting her jowls on the ledge of the tub, or sniffing under the door to try to find me, letting out sad whimpers when she ended up on the wrong side of a wall.

But as my mother struggled more and more with addiction that summer, routine in our house began to break down. Mom couldn't hold eye contact or conversations. She tumbled and stumbled around the kitchen and screamed at us if we accused her of being drunk. She served us half-frozen chicken for dinner, and smiley-faced breakfasts gave way to sleeping in and a drowsy "Come and kiss me goodbye before you and Dad head out the door." I knew that I was leaving the house at the end of the summer, but Erisy wasn't.

Erisy was my little sister and built-in best friend. Sure, she was four years younger, but people frequently mistook us for twins. We loved this and told them we were seven minutes apart. Erisy was the type of girl who mastered everything she tried. She nailed fouetté turns before I ever did, sang and played piano, taught herself guitar, always made better grades, *and* got Dad's brain in math. (I got Mom's.) Okay, fine. I was jealous. But I loved being her older sister, and I wanted be a good older sister. Maybe I could just be better at that than her.

So that summer I tried to distract her—surprising her with doughnuts in the morning, leaving little notes on her pillow, or blowing up balloons and putting them in her room for no reason. When things got really bad with Mom, I'd drive her to the mall and buy us matching sister bracelets. (We went through a lot of matching sister bracelets.) Soon Dad told us Erisy wasn't allowed to ride in the car with Mom anymore. This came as no surprise. Because of my mother's DUI, I received a hardship license when I was fifteen so I could help drive Erisy to school. We were often trying to keep Mom from driving at all by hiding her keys or disconnecting the battery.

And while chauffeur duties could have put a damper on my summer, this was absolutely not the case. We'd pile in the Jetta with the dogs and jet down Concord Road, dropping the windows of the car and blasting Justin Timberlake. Fatty took over the backseat, running from window to window, snorting and shaking her Cinnabum everywhere, trying to prop her stubby legs up on the door so she could reach her snout out into the wind, all *THIS IS THE BEST RIDE EVER!* Yoda curled up on Erisy's lap, and Gizelle made herself a spot in the backseat, right in the middle of Fatty's path. This did not stop Fatty. She barged right on over.

At first, Gizelle was a little unsure of what her strange sister was doing with her head out the window. So she'd hang back, watching Bertha's ears blowing in the wind as though thinking: *Well, if Bertha is doing it...* Then Gizelle would make her way over to the window. She'd prop the tip of her nose out into the air skeptically, constantly looking over at Fatty, then scoot her head a little farther. When the wind hit her eyes, though, she sat back in shock, blinking and shaking her head like she hated this and windows were the worst invention ever. *But if Bertha is doing it . . .* After a couple of tries, she inched her head out farther, blinking rapidly. And finally one day she went all in, thrusting her head fully into the whooshing air, eyes fluttering furiously like someone was holding a hair dryer to her face. She definitely hated it at first, but soon she loved it, because if Bertha was doing it, she would, too. True little-sister move.

Pulling the Jetta to a stop on a dusty side road overlooking the Harpeth River, Erisy and I would see who could strip down to her swimsuit faster, race to the tree, climb up, and swing off into the muddy water. Whooping, we'd jump in again and again while the dogs hung out on dry land. Once we had exhausted ourselves and cooled off, we'd load everyone back into car. We'd drop the windows again and snake around the windy hills of the South, spreading our arms out the windows to air dry. Gizelle would delightedly thump her tail in the backseat, drowned out by whooshing wind and Justin Timberlake. "Wanna go to the park?" I yelled over the music. Soon our detour turned into being gone all day. And even though Mom was unpredictable and we thought Dad had divorce in his eyes, it seemed like everything would be fine if we just drove away.

It was summertime. I was nineteen years old, and though I adored Gizelle, that never stopped me from leaving her with "Grandpa." I started spending the night out more and more, which generated texts along the following lines:

"I just fed your big puppy. Lol dad."

"Your big puppy still isn't potty trained. Lol dad."

"Your big puppy likes to get on the couch. Lol dad."

"Your big puppy likes to roll in the flowers. Lol Dad."

Dad thought "LOL" meant "lots of love," by the way. (He still does.) One day I was at the lake with friends and came out of the water to find a text saying:

"The big puppy is walking funny. Having a hard time standing up. Let me know what u want me to do. Thinking 2 call Noah's Ark. Lol Dad."

By the time I got the message, it had been a few hours since he had sent it. *Shit.*

"On my way home!" I texted from the back of a friend's truck, with a mastiff-sized ball of lead in my stomach. God, was she okay? And, am I in so much trouble? My friend stepped on the gas, but only time travel could have helped me. It was too late.

I ran into the house to see Gizelle. She wriggled and stretched out of her laundry room crate where she had been asleep and gave me a lick. "Hi, Gizelle!" Her tail knocked against the sides of her box. She seemed fine. Was Dad confused? I eyed the kitchen and the dining room for him, but he was nowhere to be seen. *Please be out playing golf. Please say you didn't call Noah's Ark.*

I ran up to my bedroom and threw my wet swimsuit on the floor to change. Then, as I was combing out my lake hair in the mirror, I heard it, the dreaded sound of his loafers clomping slowly across the floor downstairs.

I stopped, brush in hand, and stared at my reflection. "Hey, Lauren. Come downstairs for a sec," he called up to my room. This was bad. Usually I was "Fernie" or "buddy." Dad had called out "Lauren." Oh, this was so bad.

I zipped up my hoodie, twisted my hair in a towel, and crept downstairs. Dad was sitting at the kitchen table. Gizelle was plopped next to him. Bertha and Yoda lay by the windows in a patch of sun. My father didn't have to ask me to sit down; the chair was pulled out already. Dad was wearing his blue "Life Is Good" shirt, and that Life Is Good cartoon stick figure stared at me clownishly as Dad sat with his ankle over his knee and his arms crossed, bottom lip tight, frowning. Bertha and Yoda watched us, like a jury.

My heart was beating triple time in my chest. Whatever happened, I wasn't giving her back. I tried to not show that I was nervous. I sat and rested my feet on Gizelle, tracing circles in her fur with my big toe. I have my mom's big toe. It's shorter than its neighbor toe.

"I called Noah's Ark." Dad said. "Gizelle was walking funny in the backyard. Her legs were all wobbly and she was struggling to stand up. So I called to see if they could help or something." I didn't lift my head.

"They told me they don't even *have* a fostering program. They don't know a Lauren or a Gizelle." He sure had sleuthed it all out, hadn't he? I lifted my eyes to look at him but kept my chin to my chest. I tried to turn on some tears, thinking they might help around now. He stared at me with his lips pressed firmly together, waiting for me to talk. I had nothing. *Is he going to yell?* I thought, fearfully. He certainly could have. But, instead, he took a breath, and rested his elbows on his knees to level with me.

"Fernie, I don't know if honesty is important to you," he continued. "But it's important to me, and maybe Mom and I haven't done a good job of teaching it to you." (I couldn't help but think of Mom. Lies came out of her mouth as easily as hiccups.) "I want to tell you . . . " He paused. "I don't think you are going to get very far in life, or in your relationships, if you don't tell the truth." I looked up.

"Take a look at yourself, buddy," he continued. "Start thinking about the words that come out of your mouth. Don't you want to speak with integrity?"

I felt terribly embarrassed. Real tears began welling up behind my eyes.

I should have been yelled at and grounded. He should have given Gizelle away. But this was more powerful. He chose not to yell. He spoke to me like I was a grown-up. Which made sense because technically I was supposed to be one soon.

"Sorry," I said. My voice may have cracked. I looked my father in the eye and said it again. "I'm sorry."

"One thing is for sure," Dad said, reaching down to Gizelle, who was now sprawled across the floor. "I know you love your big puppy. "

He gave Gizelle two reassuring pats on the head as

though she had been his detective partner in catching me, and left the room.

I sat in the chair for a moment and looked down at Gizelle. *Does this mean we are keeping her?* I wondered. If Dad was leaning that way, the pressure was on me to not mess up. My own mom wasn't around to help anymore. She had gone to rehab for twenty-eight days, at least. Fingers crossed, she would stay the twenty-eight days and get sober. She'd be my mom again, and in the meantime, I'd be Gizelle's.

My first lesson as dog-mom came pretty fast, because Dad hadn't been mistaken about Gizelle's funny walk. One evening, soon after I'd been busted in the big foster puppy lie, the house was Mom-less and quiet, and Dad was getting ready to grill steaks for me, Erisy, and Tripp and his new wife, Jenna. I walked barefoot into the yard to find Gizelle sitting in the grass. "Come here, Gizelle!" I said, patting my thighs so she'd play with me. She tried to get up, but it looked as though her paws were chained to the ground. She wobbled awkwardly, as if her legs were suddenly lame. "Dad!" I yelled.

"Yeah?" He opened the door and saw Gizelle wriggling in the grass.

"Yeah, that's what she was doing before. I don't know what's wrong with her."

"We have to take her to the vet!" Dad put the steaks back in the fridge, and the team rallied. All of us—Dad, Tripp, Jenna, Erisy, and I went to the after-hours vet. We huddled in the little room, surrounding Gizelle. They put a thermometer in Gizelle's behind, checked her ears, looked in her nose, pulled on her tail and stretched each of her limbs. Nothing. It cost five hundred dollars that night to figure out that Gizelle had "growing pains." Yup, just growing pains. "This is common in giant breed dogs," the vet assured. The five of us stood, relieved. The vet looked puzzled by the sight of so many of us crammed in this one room for growing pains. Well, now we knew what it was. But I discovered something else that night, looking at my family packed in this tiny room circled around Gizelle, each of us stroking her ears and rubbing her tummy and gazing at her with love and Dad covering the vet bill without complaint. We were totally keeping the big puppy.

3

Making Lists

Summer was over and I was staring out the eleventh-floor window of a colossal and intimidating fourteen-floor sorority dorm. My new home. The hallways were filled with colorful Greek letters. Rooms had matching Lilly Pulitzer bedding and monogrammed laundry hampers. Girls walked around arm in arm in shirts that said things like, "Pi or Die," and everything seemed to match, match, match.

Trying to adapt to the whole Greek life thing as a transfer sorority girl was tough. Leaving Gizelle and Erisy was tougher. I did my best to fit in at my new school. I went to a formal, tailgated at a football game, wrapped myself in a bedsheet for a toga party (*and* threw up on the lawn). *Do I fit in yet? Do I* want *to fit in?* I wondered. But when 6:30 p.m. Monday night rolled around, when all my sisters primped and polished and flooded the eleventh-floor hallway to march down the hill to the weekly Chapter meeting, I stayed behind. I don't think anyone noticed.

I had transferred from the College of Charleston in South Carolina to be closer to Erisy during her last three years of high school. So I went home most weekends. Every time I walked through the door, the big puppy was bigger. Soon she was bigger than me, and she wasn't finished growing.

Of course, Gizelle wasn't aware she was nearing the size of a La-Z-Boy chair. In her mind she was no bigger than Yoda. She would army-crawl under short coffee tables to take a nap. Inevitably the table would tilt up over her head. She was our resident bulldozer, spilling coffee and knocking over frames with her tail. And if my sister and I were snuggled on the small two-person love seat in the living room watching a movie, Gizelle was blind to the fact that there wasn't space for her, too. She would always make room, stealthily placing one paw up and then another paw. Then a graceful launch of all 100-something pounds of her right into our laps. Crushing our thighs and bellies, blocking our view, and pinning our arms to our sides, she would open her mouth to a light, smiley pant, almost as if she thought: *They do not even know I am here.*

As Gizelle kept growing, Mom's pupils kept shrinking. She returned from rehab and twenty-eight days of forced sobriety and within minutes took off in her car. My family fell back into the same old traps, following her around, digging through her closet, calling liquor stores to see if she'd visited.

One weekend I came home to find her passed out on the couch at 5 p.m. There was a new dent in her car, mini Sutter Home bottles hidden away in the depths of her closet, and Tylenol bottles filled with colorful pills I did not think were Tylenol. I decided to confront her. "Mom." I tried to speak calmly. "Why are you taking these? What are these for?" I held the pills out in front of her. She squinted at my hand, then stared off into space, like her words were lost, floating around in her head, and she had to find them first. After a moment she turned back to me, "I'm not, sweetie! I'm not taking those anymore. I'm totally fine!" she insisted, baffled that I would accuse her of such a thing.

There had been times she had been convincing, times

I'd start to battle my own brain, wondering if I was the crazy one for saying "Mom isn't fine." I wrestled briefly with that thought, remembering how she had just mailed me a new purse and months before had spoiled me with the giant puppy. But looking back into my mother's glassy eyes, I snapped back into reality.

"No. Mom. You are not fine. You are lying!"

She glared at me, but struggled to hold eye contact. As my words registered, anger broke through her drowsy stupor, and she snapped. "How could you not believe me? It's so unfair! After all I do for you!" Suddenly, we were storming through the house like two teenagers, slamming cabinets and yelling as loud as we could in the same-old you-have-a-problem-no-I-don't-have-a-problem argument until I finally called Dad to yell at him, too. "Dad! We cannot live like this! It's not fair. It's not fair to Erisy! Why aren't you *doing* something? Please, *please* make her leave!" And this is why addiction is the knottiest, meanest, most confusing illness. It messes with everyone involved. It's a bully.

I was losing my mom to that bully.

I slammed the door of my car and drove away from my house with Gizelle. I didn't just want to leave Brentwood, I wanted to run away from Tennessee entirely. I hated school and hated home and did not know where I belonged. We had tried everything with Mom. I thought if I could catch her in her lies, if I could make her admit she had a problem, if I pleaded, tried to reason with her—something would work. *Something* had to work. . . . Right? I was trembling with rage. I slapped my hands against the steering wheel. "Fuck!" I yelled, flying up I-65 north toward Nashville as Gizelle shifted in the backseat to rest her chin on the center console, still trying to be as close to me as possible. I tried to take deep breaths. I tried to calm myself down. But I could not understand why my mother would keep choosing the pills and the alcohol over her family. (And she did, eventually, choose the pills and alcohol over her family. Later, Dad would tell Mom she had to move out if she refused to seek help. She didn't put up much of a fight. She just left.)

I drove until I reached Percy Warner Park. The Warner Parks are southwest of Nashville and have more than two thousand acres of hilly trail. I needed air. I found a random trail, clipped on Gizelle's leash, and started walking. Gizelle stayed right with me. Not behind me. Not pulling out in front of me. Beside me. She was a natural on her leash. As we made our way up the path, she kept looking up at me. She sometimes did this as visual confirmation I was with her, but that day I felt she sensed my distress. We walked faster, and soon our trot turned to a jog. Gizelle trotted just beside me. Then she started getting faster. We picked up speed. Our six feet beat together like two drums.

The leash flapped between us. Obviously, a leash is made to bind human and dog, and I've often felt it to be a nice connector, something that made me and Gizelle feel like two parts of one whole. Yet, at that moment, the leash felt like it was in the way, tangling the air between us. Making things knotty.

So, I took the leash off, and we ran.

We ran next to each other. A mini stampede. We were completely in sync, and not thinking about much but the present moment. We ran as fast as we could as the trees *whooshed* by. Gizelle came up to my hips, but she never tried to jump in front of me or nip at my feet like a lot of dogs would. Her jowls flapped in the wind and her long pink tongue flailed happily out of her mouth as she ran next to me. Like a protector. Like a friend. Then it didn't even seem like we were two drums. We were one massive drum beating loudly with every step. *Boom. Boom. Boom. Boom.*

We ran for a few minutes until we found a clearing and fell down onto the grass. I rested my head on her stomach and listened to her panting slowly subside along with my own. I couldn't believe I had a massive dog who would follow me without a leash. She followed me just because she wanted to be with me. My head moved on her belly with her slowing breath. Then Gizelle turned around and licked my face followed by a nibble on my nose. This was how she told me she loved me.

I kept running through college. Running gave me a purpose when I wasn't sure what my purpose was. I felt grounded, connected to the earth. I wasn't fighting parts of my life that were distressing. Running was the first thing I can remember doing in my life where I felt like I was actually doing exactly what I was supposed to be doing.

Running also made me feel productive, like I was taking

advantage of my days and pushing myself to do something physically and mentally demanding. And as I watched my mom doing the opposite, sleeping her life away and losing days, I found myself afraid of being like her. I didn't want to miss out on life. I wanted to show up for it. So I started training for my first half marathon. Gizelle became my training partner.

Having a 160-pound English mastiff training partner had its limitations and was not without risk. One pretty afternoon in late spring, I took Gizelle and Bertha to the park at the Brentwood YMCA—planning to do sprints on the soccer field. Usually Gizelle would do a little running around with me, but Bertha's shorter physique wasn't built for much activity. I didn't have the heart to bench Fatty alone because that might make her feel self-conscious, so I leashed both girls to a nearby soccer goal. Gizelle lay in a sphinx position, watching me, and Fatty rolled over on her back, snorting in the grass.

With that, I took off running. Gizelle's ears lifted and her eyes followed me intently as I ran back and forth across the field. On my third sprint back toward the goal, I gave Gizelle a little pat on the head. She must have taken this as a *You coming or not?* Because when I took off, Gizelle took off, too, dragging the soccer goal and poor Fatty along with her—an unlikely threesome careening across the field. Gizelle didn't realize that *she* was the one towing a soccer goal along; she only saw a big net chasing her. She ran faster *from* the goal, with poor Bertha's stubby legs scurrying at maximum new speeds trying to keep up. I rerouted myself completely to run after them, laughing and screaming and flailing my arms. Once I finally caught up, it took more than a minute to wrangle the tangle of dogs from the soccer goal in front of a parking lot full of howling children and soccer moms.

Eventually Gizelle came to live with me in Knoxville. We'd run through campus together at night, trotting down Sixteenth Street, past my old sorority dorm, and onto Volunteer Boulevard, where the campus sidewalk sloped upward into a grassy hill near the library. Every time we approached this spot, Gizelle began walking with purpose, picking up speed, tapping her front paws on the concrete with excitement. "Ready, girl? Ready?" I'd unhook the leash.

There weren't many students out, but the ones who were would always stop in their tracks, books in hand, struck by the sight of the huge dog on campus running through the shadows. As she ran up the hill, she always turned her head around to make sure I was following. I'd chase after her, and together we'd dart into the grass, side by side underneath a sky full of stars.

Nights on campus with Gizelle always got me thinking. If I could say I wanted to run one mile, and then run that one mile, what else could I do if I set my mind to it? Where else could my feet take me? When I ran, I started dreaming of the places I wanted to go, the things I wanted to see, and what kind of person I wanted to be once I got there. I started listing items in my head, writing them in journals:

Run a whole marathon
See the lions in Africa
Study abroad
Eat pizza in Italy
Fall in love
Get a tattoo

This list eventually earned the title "Lauren's Bucket List." I crossed off and added things as I went.

~~Run a whole marathon~~
~~Study abroad~~
~~Get a tattoo~~
~~Be an au-pair in Italy~~
~~Eat pizza in Italy~~
~~Eat gelato in Italy~~
~~Eat Spaghetti alla Carbonera in Italy~~

Soon I was twenty-three, out of college and wondering what was next for me. My parents had separated and would soon divorce. Erisy had left for college in California. Tripp and Jenna moved to LA. Mom checked herself back into rehab. Friends were nailing internships, starting careers, or getting married. As I scanned my list, there was one item that felt like it was practically glowing on the page. One item that seemed like the most logical next step in life, even though I had no idea what I was doing with my life.

I decided I would move away from Tennessee. I would trade my life in the South for a place a little more energetic, gritty, cosmopolitan. A place I knew almost nothing about. I was going to move to New York City. To Manhattan. And Gizelle was coming with me.

4

Manhattan

43rd Street, Times Square

While I continued to work on my bucket list, thrilled to soon cross off "Live in Manhattan," Gizelle continued to work on a list of her own. Her list of fears. Gizelle was terrified of nearly everything.

Mailboxes

Drains

Strangers

Yoda

Cardboard boxes and pots

Soccer goals (rightfully so!)

Bikes

Bertha

Plastic bags

Power tools

The bike didn't even have to be moving. Once there was a bicycle on the floor of the garage and Gizelle crept around it so carefully you'd think it was a grizzly bear she was trying not to wake. Another time she refused to go out into the yard because there was a vicious plastic bag out there blowing in the wind. And it only took Yoda one snarly snap for Gizelle to retreat under the table all *Gee, I'm so sorry, Yoda! Please don't hurt me!*

So, naturally, bringing my massive baby to New York City, a place where I was certain we would come across more plastic bags blowing in the wind, bicycles, drains, and (larger and louder) power tools and machinery—I was slightly apprehensive. Sure, Gizelle had become bolder and more confident during her time at the University of Tennessee, but my girl still put the gentle in gentle giant. What if Manhattan terrified Gizelle? What if she arrived and immediately wanted to country-roads-take-me-home, back to a land of quiet starry nights and grassy fields and car rides? There was only one way to find out. And it began with finding us an apartment.

For an outsider, finding a home in New York City is the city's first test. It's New York's way of saying, *So, how badly do you want to live here? How much of your space, moral compass, income, tolerance of filth, and dignity will you sacrifice? How insane are you?* It's survival of the fittest. If you can't handle the apartment hunt, maybe you shouldn't stay. Maybe New York City is not the best match for you. Which, in a way, I like, because that means people who live here must technically, somewhere deep down, want to live here, or else you would never torture yourself with the pain-in-the-ass apartment hunt. I soon felt that all of Manhattan worked this way—if you weren't willing to work, it would eat you alive, but if you were, and if fate would cooperate, there were rewards.

One of the biggest gifts fate bestowed was Kimmy. Kimmy was from Hartford, Connecticut, but had gone to school in New Jersey. I'd met her studying abroad in college and we became instant friends. Kimmy was one of four sisters, and she had the same my-closet-is-your-closet outlook as me. She was the type of girl whom a number of people would count as their best friend.

That first year we lived together, she was a bridesmaid or maid of honor in about twelve different weddings. Once a month, like clockwork, she'd be gluing rhinestones in cursive on a sailor hat (Brides Mate!) for *another* bachelorette party, then she'd look at me and roll her eyes and say, "Fuck. These. Weddings," then laugh and get right back to her rhinestones.

We both couldn't believe people our age were getting married. Moving to New York City and having a dog was the biggest commitment we both wanted to make. We were twenty-three and saw the city as one giant playground. Girls our age? Settling down? *Now?* But there was still so much to see and do and explore! Kimmy and I had already done a lot of exploring together, too. We bungee jumped off the highest bungee bridge in the world, did a homestay in Nagano, slept on canoes for no reason, and now we were taking on New York City for our greatest adventure yet.

As we walked to meet our broker, I asked Kimmy if there was anything that bothered her about roommates, and she just said, "Ugh. Living with people who get mad about stupid shit." That made sense to me. Who wants to be around those people? Right? But wait a minute: *Do I get mad about stupid shit?* I didn't think so. Studying abroad, Kimmy had earned the nickname Farm Girl, because she was always drinking a lot and saying funny, dirty things and posing provocatively in front of important historical monuments. But that never bothered me; I was usually right there alongside her!

I adored Kimmy. She was easygoing yet motivated, never

picky, and truly selfless. The girl could survive on condiments alone if she needed to. Once, when I was hungry, she gave me her bag of chips and ate a packet of ketchup instead, just squirted it into her mouth. "What? It's good!" she claimed. The other thing about Kimmy was that she was thrilled to have a dog. "I've never had a dog before! Always wanted one!" she cheered. She'd met Gizelle once before in Knoxville. Her reaction? "Oh, she doesn't even seem that big!" Yes, Kimmy was perfect roommate material. If only we could find an apartment.

We found a broker named Allie who led us up what felt like every staircase in Hell's Kitchen, a neighborhood she claimed was "affordable." Despite all those stairs, Allie was a devoted fan of the pencil skirt. We followed those pencil skirts through a number of "sundrenched," "modern," "huge" apartments. But the places we saw were tiny—so small that *if* there was room for a couch, you could reach the fridge from it. It didn't take long to discover that being able to even fit a bed in a bedroom was a luxury and having a window facing the smallest sliver of sun was a miracle. *And what about dogs? Where do New Yorkers put dogs?* I wondered. Gizelle hadn't arrived in New York City just yet. In fact, she would only arrive if I had a place to put her. But some of the apartments were so small that I doubted Kimmy, Gizelle, and I could all fit in the place at the same time. Gizelle would have to walk out into the hallway to turn around.

Needless to say, despite lovable, our third roommate was not an asset to the search.

"How much does your dog weigh again? You said she was bigger, right?" Allie asked, leading us to potential new home number seventeen, another "total steal."

I didn't want to tell the real estate agent how big Gizelle actually was. I even left her weight blank on the paperwork. Like a lot of girls, Gizelle's weight fluctuated. She was a little bigger than usual at this point—the biggest she'd ever be. This may have been partly because when I left to study abroad Gizelle was left doing lots of studying the couch and not getting quite as much exercise as she had with me. So when I returned, myself with puffy pain-au-chocolat cheeks, another chin, and a new Nutella crepe belly, I was not alone in newfound surface area. Gizelle's voluptuous curves were no longer, and she had entered what Tripp called "Gizelle's Bathtub Phase." My girl was about 180 pounds.

"Umm. She's just over a hundred pounds," I told Allie when she asked directly. Sorry, but everyone has to lie about her weight at some point. Allie's eyes widened, her nostrils flared, and she shook her head. "Oh, well, a dog that size is really going to limit you," she warned in a parental tone, shuffling through the papers on her clipboard. She didn't know the half of it. Truly, there was a whole other half of Gizelle that Pencil Skirt didn't know existed. I didn't feel that bad lying to Allie about Gizelle's weight. Allie kept lying to us, too. Allie kept telling us her apartments were affordable and large and sunny. These apartments were none of those things.

I began to despair. I was trying not to be picky. I didn't

need a big, sprawling house, and neither did Kimmy. Neither did Gizelle, come to think of it. A small apartment would probably be Gizelle's dream, as my lap still seemed to be her most desired residence.

So Kimmy and I kept looking for a small but livable apartment. And just as I was about to decide this New York City apartment hunt was one terrible tragedy, we followed Allie into an apartment on Forty-Third between Eighth and Ninth Avenues.

She flipped on the light.

My mouth fell open in amazement. I couldn't believe my eyes. There was room for a couch and a chair and a TV and a large dog, *and* there was a separate kitchen. We didn't own furniture, but it was nice to know that if we did, there would be a place to put it. There were two bedrooms, and a private wooden patio out back with a fence around it. It was a miraculous discovery. Allie kept looking down at her clipboard then back up at the apartment in shock, and I worried she'd made a mistake and shown us a place that wasn't in our price range. But there was no mistake.

One of the rooms was significantly bigger than the other, and I thought Kimmy and I might fight over it. "You can have the bigger one," Kimmy said, totally unconcerned. "You have the pup!" There was even a tree on this back patio. Yes, a tree. Okay, the tree was growing from somewhere underneath the back bedroom, and the roots did push that bedroom floor into a slope, and sometimes when it was windy I was scared the tree would fall and uproot the entire place and we'd fly away like Dorothy. But there was a tree! A tree to remind me of Tennessee. The last tenant had even left white Christmas lights strung across the fence, a couple of lanterns, and flower pots for a garden. I could put a hammock back there. There was enough room for Gizelle to lie in the sun. A license plate that said RIO hung on the wooden fence from some twine. And, just like that, our first apartment in New York City had a name.

Kimmy and I decorated Rio by browsing the sidewalks of Hell's Kitchen. Our apartment was like a shelter for stray and abandoned furniture. We took it all: poor, tired, broken chairs, a countertop down on its luck that we painted black and used as a bar, a rolling side table in need of a new home. Kimmy's dad even found a couch on the street by their house in Hartford after a rainstorm. It was nothing short of hideous—olive green and still damp. We didn't care. We took that, too. We marched it to the back of Rio's patio and it became affectionately known as Swamp Thang. In the kitchen, Kimmy hung the corkboard we'd bought from Jack's 99 Cent Store. "Nothing cheesy," she said. "None of that Live, Laugh, Love crap in this apartment."

We splurged on chalkboard paint so that we could color and write important stuff on the walls. Lists. "Buy shower curtain," I wrote. It took us about a week to get that done; in the meantime water just spilled to the floor and you took your steps carefully after getting out of the shower. "Get grown-up jobs," we wrote. We both already had restaurant jobs. My older cousin had hooked me up with a job at a bar on the Upper West Side before I'd even arrived in New

York so that I could have an immediate source of income, and Kimmy was a waitress at a gastropub in Murray Hill. In a few weeks we would write the best message of all: "Welcome to New York, Gizelle!"

It seemed like a good omen: an empty parking spot for Mom right in front of my apartment. Mom was out of rehab and living in a town house in Nashville and seemed to be doing well. Lately, when she and I spoke on the phone, her voice was crisper and more clear. She called to check up on me more often, and I told her all about my new Times Square apartment. She asked if she could please drive Gizelle to me, so we could have "Mommy-Lauren" time. She missed me. Still, it was never easy to figure out how she was really doing, but her wanting to visit me seemed like a great sign. She asked if I could email her a list of the things I wanted from my old room and she would drive them to me. *My mom is back!* I hoped, feeling lucky that I had a mother who would offer to do these things for me.

Gizelle jumped out of my mom's SUV, first dropping her front paws on the sidewalk, then lugging her hefty second half out of the car. She wasn't always the fastest-moving dog, but when she saw me, her ears perked forward, her eyes widened, and she started jumping up and down with her front paws. I did not keep it cool, either. "Gizelle!" I gasped, "Hi! Hi, my girl! Hi!" I wrapped my arms around her neck as she nibbled my nose on the sidewalk of Forty-Third. "I missed you!" She did a few more excited circles in front of me, then kept jumping her front paws in the air while I swatted them with my hands.

"Hi, Mom!" I said, running to hug her next, a little nervous to see her. *What if her eyes are foggy? What if she's slurring her words?* I trusted her to drive Gizelle all the way to New York, but my biggest fear was still Mom driving under the influence. Sure, a part of me knew if she wasn't doing well, she probably wouldn't have offered to make the long trip to New York in the first place. When she wasn't doing well, she seemed to try to avoid seeing us. But when I saw my mother rush toward me, her eyes brightening as she opened her arms to hug me and her face breaking into an enormous smile, my shoulders relaxed. Mom squeezed me tight. Her car was filled with my things—my big map of the world, Gizelle's dog bed, my little Buddha statue, a suitcase stuffed with books.

I pointed out our building. "Oh my gosh, I love your home, sweetie!" Mom gasped, pinching my hand as she smiled and looked up at the apartment. The building had a cracked front door, which had been duct-taped and graf-fitied, and a buzzer that buzzed at random without being pressed. The hallway had blinking fluorescent lights that gave it a horror-movie murder-scene feel. "I'm so happy for you!" Mom said. "It's magical."

And that was also how I knew my mother was doing well: she thought my rundown apartment across from the Port Authority Bus Terminal was magical. When she was sober, I swear the woman could find the beauty in anything.

Seeing Gizelle, my mom, and my stuff sitting in laundry baskets on the sidewalk made me realize that this move was real and permanent . . . at least as permanent as things get for a twenty-three-year-old.

I couldn't believe it—Gizelle and I were living in the middle of Manhattan, a little over a block away from Madame Tussauds wax museum, and (most conveniently) right next to the Times Square 99 Cent Express Pizza joint. Our local Walgreens pharmacy sign flickered in flashy, impressive red neon. And I needed no reminder that I♥NYC, because it was written all over thousands of knickknacks in tourist shops that lined Eighth Avenue. Mom and I gathered up the laundry baskets and we all trekked into Rio.

Mom stayed for a couple of days. She took Kimmy and me to Anthony Bourdain's restaurant, Les Halles. I was pleased when my mother ordered water but insisted Kimmy and I order a celebratory glass of champagne. The next day Mom drove us to Ikea, where Kimmy and I were entirely too ambitious in thinking that our apartment was a palace and bought a shelf that was way too big for the living room. We attempted putting it together, piece by piece, blocking Gizelle into the hallway until we finally realized this shelf was never going to fit. "No worries, girls." Mom smiled as she helped us take the shelf apart. Then she drove us right back to Ikea the next day.

Arm in arm, Mom and I walked Gizelle briefly around the block. "Let's not overdo it with her, sweetie," she warned, explaining that since we didn't want gentle Gizelle to go into sensory overload, we should introduce her to city life slowly. I agreed. On my mom's last night in New York, Gizelle and I walked her to her hotel a couple of blocks away. "Thanks for everything, Mommy," I said, hugging her tight. I released my grasp and her eyes lingered for a moment on the lights behind me. "Mom?" Then she shifted her eyes to me. "You okay?" I asked. She paused for a moment.

"Of course." She kissed my cheek again and disappeared into the hotel. I couldn't help but wonder what my mother was going to do when she got upstairs to her hotel room, or worse, back to her apartment in Nashville where she was all alone.

5

Times Scare

Journaling on Rio's rooftop; New York, New York

Regardless of Mom's state of recovery or lack thereof, it was incredible she had brought me Gizelle. Plus, Gizelle and I were city girls now. We were on our own. Maybe it was time to put aside the addiction concerns I had with my mother. I was in New York City! I had my best friend with me now. It was November. Time to explore.

I wrapped Gizelle's pink leather leash around my hand to keep her close to my knee, praying she wouldn't tuck her tail and crouch toward the sidewalk, pulling away from the honking taxies, loud subway grates, and high-speed rolling Nuts 4 Nuts carts that I occasionally found myself ducking away from. "You got this, girl," I coached. We walked across town on Forty-Third Street to Bryant Park, and much to my surprise, Gizelle *did* have this. Gizelle didn't duck away from Manhattan; she merged onto the sidewalk, which was more of a freeway of people, and remained by my side. Her hips shifted as she walked. She didn't stop and stand in place. She wasn't distracted by the motion and noise around us. Gizelle walked on casually, not paying attention to anything or anyone, like a true New Yorker. *Gizelle? How are you doing this?* I thought, wishing she'd give me pointers on how to look more city girl. So far it seemed as though Gizelle could handle Manhattan, but it didn't take long for me to start wondering if Manhattan could handle Gizelle.

When we crossed Forty-Third and Broadway at Times Square, Gizelle scared Batman. As we approached, Bruce Wayne pulled his bat cape around him and tucked his pillow-stuffed muscle chest behind a guy dressed as his thug rival, Bane. "Aw, shit! That's a big-ass dog!" Batman cursed. Gotham was in serious trouble.

Gizelle and I parted a sea of cartoon characters—Hello Kitty, Elmo, Buzz Lightyear, the Pink Power Ranger, Mario and Luigi, all of whom marched around the busy pedestrian walkway much like Batman did, in costumes that looked a little like they came from Party City. And much like Batman did, the cartoons would all step back and point, sometimes lifting their masks, sweaty red faces exposed, watching Gizelle in wonder as if she were a superpower they hadn't yet contended with.

Longtime local the Naked Cowboy, known for busking in nothing but tighty-whities and cowboy boots, looked down at my huge brindle and then back up at me, dumbfounded, as though I were the crazy one. *Sir, it's November,* I wanted to point out. *You're standing in Times Square in your skivvies playing guitar. She's only a dog.*

I always envisioned New Yorkers rushing past one another on the streets. I pictured them in black business suits, focused, serious, and oblivious to everything but their own agenda. Well, that was not our experience. When people saw Gizelle on the sidewalks of Hell's Kitchen, they seemed to lose control over their emotions. They'd broadcast whatever came to mind.

"That is not a dog, that's Jumanji."

"Cujo!"

"Holy shit!"

"YOU CRAZY!"

"Lion!"

"Tiger!"

"Whoa!"

It was almost as though guessing Gizelle's species were a parlor game, like charades or celebrity, in which passersby had to blurt out an answer as fast as they could.

"The Beast!"

"Mufasssaaaaaa!"

"Godzilla!"

"Sandlot!"

"Beowulf!" (Grendel?)

"A bear!"

"Whoa!"

People loved telling me that Gizelle was anything but a dog. One guy outside a deli on Eighth Avenue tapped me with one finger to let me know, politely, carefully and with utter assurance, "I would like to let you know, that is not a dog. That is a Tyrannosaurus Rex." It was clear that he was trying to help me out. He wanted to make sure I knew I was actually walking a fierce carnivorous lizard from the late Cretaceous Period so that I would take the necessary precautions.

Sometimes people also took the trouble to point out to me that Gizelle was, indeed, a dog. But in this scenario, it was usually sandwiched somewhere in the middle of the words, "Holy shit! That's a big fuckin' dog!"

It was as if no one had ever seen a dog before, which was bizarre because this neighborhood had a lot of them. "How do you have that dog in the city?" "Where do you live?" "How big is your apartment?" people asked, paparazzi style. Sometimes people with bigger dogs, like Labs or golden retrievers, would stop and ask the same thing, "Oh my god! How on earth do you fit that in an apartment?" And this was always very funny to me because, as I looked down, it was *their* lab that was practically doing a River Dance, running in circles, tangled up in the leash or jumping up and down on two legs for a ball in the owner's hand, while Gizelle, who got sick of standing in one place, was usually lying on the sidewalk by that time. She was impossible to keep clean. A layer of city grime clung to her beautiful brindle coat every time we left the house. This layer of grime sometimes found its way to my bedsheets. Needless to say, bath time became more of a priority than ever before. Gizelle being allowed on the sheets also became much more regulated with that bath-time schedule.

Gizelle's poo situation didn't help with any efforts to blend in. They brought her more attention than I ever would have wished. I'd watch the small-dog owners plucking, with two fingers, their pup's tiny number twos in what I could only assume were pink watermelon-scented bags, while I used produce bags I'd hijacked from Trader Joe's, hoping two would be enough and praying for no plastic malfunctions. There were sometimes malfunctions. Maybe a shovel would have been easier. In Tennessee, Gizelle droppings didn't have an audience. I'd clean it up from a quiet green park, plunk it in a trash bin, and no big deal. "It's like it didn't even happen, girl," I'd assure her.

Now that Gizelle had to go on Manhattan's busy side-walks in front of large crowds, there was nowhere to hide. People held their noses as they passed and someone, with-out fail, would always wind up calling out, "Gross!"

Perhaps this is why it took Gizelle a week to work up the courage to go in Manhattan in the first place. On walks, Gizelle stared at me like I was crazy for actually thinking she was going to use the busy, scent-filled sidewalk as a potty, like all the other city dogs. I imagined she felt like girls do when they need to go at a new boyfriend's, or in a Bonnaroo porta potty—you're most likely just not going to do it. You can't. You'll wait. But I don't think Gizelle got that she couldn't just wait. Bonnaroo was home now.

A week passed. I grew worried. I called her vet. I googled "My dog won't shit" and "How to make your dog go on concrete." We'd walk around Hell's Kitchen to Bryant Park, to private parking lots where she could be shielded by cars, to the waterfront by the West Side Highway, but Gizelle only sniffed. I had a strong urge to let her consecrate the no-dogs Bryant Park lawn if exclusivity was what she needed, but we refrained. Then, one day, the job fell to Kimmy.

Kimmy and Gizelle were on Forty-Third Street and Tenth Avenue near a Dunkin' Donuts, a favorite spot of Kimmy's, being from Boston and all. In a hurry, Kimmy had chosen to tempt fate and not bring a Trader Joe's doggy poop bag with her, a monumentally bad decision. Gizelle had waited long enough. All of a sudden, she halted on the busy sidewalk and squatted. After a week of not going, Kimmy said it was so big it could have shaken the Empire

State Building. People dodged the massive pile with horror as Kimmy stood there, empty-handed, arms out like a soccer goalie trying to stop people from stepping in it, unsure what to do. So, she held her breath, dug out an extra-large, bucket-sized Dunkin' Donuts iced coffee cup from a pile of trash to scoop it up and then placed Gizelle's copious work on an already overflowing trash bin. Then she immediately texted: "OMG! Gizelle pooped! And holy shit! Giz's shits are huge." I sent her back poo emojis and celebration confetti emojis and we both wondered if this was how it felt when your toddler grew up to win the Nobel Prize.

There is a reason Times Square is called the Crossroads of the World. Over 300,000 pedestrians walk through it every day. There seemed to be every type of human in one place, and Gizelle and I lived among them, in what sometimes felt like living in a combination of Las Vegas and Disney World. Sometimes it felt like we'd tumbled down a well and woken up in this strange land filled with the sounds of taxi horns and jackhammers and a whole lotta people. Which was ironic, because that's exactly what happens in *Enchanted*, the movie whose protagonist Gizelle is named for. Naive Princess Giselle (Amy Adams) is pushed down a well by an evil queen and falls from her perfect, cartoon fairy-tale world and ends up trapped in real life. In Times Square, actually.

I quickly understood why people called New York City a jungle, because jungles are filled with the most exotic creatures. Thanks to Gizelle, I met many of them. One of my favorites was our zany flyer guy friend, who stood on the corner of Forty-Third Street and Eighth Avenue, wearing a sign for Diamond gentlemen's club. Bespectacled, fiftyish, with hair that looked as though he enjoyed experimenting with electricity, our conversations tended to run as follows:

"Ohhh hey, Gizelle! Hey!" He never failed to greet her, which was always in the middle of a busy workday for him. He'd wave his hands in the air excitedly; there was never any passing without stopping. He'd lean over and pet Gizelle, eyes big behind his glasses, and she'd wag her tail politely. "How are *you*, Gizelle? How you ladies doing?"

"We're good," I'd say, answering for Gizelle as usual. "How are you?"

"Oh, I'm good . . . Free strippers! Lap dances! . . . " He'd call out, midconversation, flyers in his hand.

" . . . things are good. Just working, paying bills . . . Naked ladies! Classy girls!" Someone snatched a flyer with a bodacious half-naked, Kardashian type on it and he was quick to hold up another.

"You ladies going to the park?"

"Yeah, we're just going for a little run-walk, getting some fresh air."

"Strippers! Exotic strippers! . . . That's just great. I love the fresh air, too."

I smiled and nodded in agreement.

"Okay, well, enjoy your evening, ladies. See you tomorrow I hope. Bye, Gizelle . . . Strippers! Hot, sexy girls!"

He and I never knew so much as each other's names—it would have broken a code between New Yorkers to be so presumptuous as to ask any personal details of each other. But he knew Gizelle's. We talked almost every day, he rubbed Gizelle's head just right, and she liked him, sometimes even resting her chin on his knee while he tousled her ears. I liked him, too. And I wouldn't have ever had reason to speak to him if it weren't for Gizelle. The whole thing made me wonder if I could officially cross "strangers" off Gizelle's list of fears.

Another favorite exchange occurred when we ran into a guy who looked like John Candy, wearing a black *Phantom of the Opera* T-shirt topped with an unbuttoned red Hawaiian shirt. I bumped into him outside of the Shake Shack on Eighth Avenue. He studied Gizelle with a few curious looks before addressing her, "Well, hello, big puppy!" (We liked him immediately.)

He looked back up at me.

"May I pet your dog?"

"Of course!" I walked closer.

For a moment his hands squeezed into fists with excitement before he bent down to pet Gizelle on the head.

"What is the doggy's name?" he asked, looking at her tenderly.

"Gizelle," I beamed.

His mouth silently dropped open. "Oh my GOD. GIZELLE? From *Enchanted*?" His voice got higher with each exclamation. I smiled. "Yeah! You know it? People never know it."

He clapped his hands together with recognition.

"Ohmigod. *Girl*. I know it."

And what happened next was nothing less than cinematic. The man curtseyed at Gizelle, a beautiful, balletic curtsey, and then began to sing Amy Adams's "Happy Working Song" from *Enchanted*. He spun and twirled on the sidewalk as people zipped by. Pedestrians stared at Gizelle as they passed but completely ignored the dancing maestro of Disney lyrics. I swung Gizelle's leash in time to his song, certain this was the type of thing that could only happen in New York City, also certain that we were definitely in the movie *Enchanted* and really had fallen down a well to an eccentric, wonderful land where people like him existed.

Even though Gizelle seemed like a New York natural, I often wondered how she was feeling about her new life. Was she comfortable here? Did she feel out of place? Despite seeming pretty content, there were certain things that still scared her, like buses. She would never get over the buses. She'd back away slowly as the M20 *vroomed* up Eighth Avenue, then the moment the bus stopped and the air brakes made that loud *Kssssh* sound she'd dive toward the buildings, hugging her big body tight against the walls, tugging me along with her. I still wince at the sound of bus's air brakes today. "It's okay, girl, don't worry," I'd soothe, stopping to rub her ears and calm her down until she'd shake off her fear, and we'd carry on through the neighborhood.

Sometimes our neighborhood freaked me out, too. We lived next to a place called the Times Scare, which was New York City's only year-round haunted house. So, if the guys wheeling hot dog carts at warp speed weren't enough, or the thousands of tourists staring into their SLR cameras, the street artists shilling CDs, the guy chasing you for "free hugs," or the people cursing at me and Gizelle—on top of that, there were also people dressed as zombies. They roamed our street with bloody gashes and bite marks painted on their faces, growling and snorting at tourists year-round to advertise that haunted house. Given where Gizelle and I had grown up, a Nashville suburb so quiet that families of deer and wild turkeys came to graze in our backyard, the Times Square community was an interesting and sometimes frightening new normal.

Often we walked across Forty-Third Street to the Hudson River for fresh air, next to a dog park that looked like nothing more than a few parking spaces with a fence around it. I would press my body against the railing that lined the Hudson and look out onto the water. The earthy, salty, tang of garbage mixed with river entered my nose, and I was reminded that I was living on an island, and I couldn't decide if we were both trapped on it like the dogs in the dog park or if we were thriving in the City of Dreams with the whole world at our fingertips: strippers, zombies, and everything in between.

A friend once told me that New York City was the only place where you could travel the world without leaving the city's borders, and I hoped this was true, because Gizelle and I were going to remain here, carless, conspicuous, and curious. The only other home we'd known was hundreds of miles away in Tennessee. We had our first grown-up apartment, a lease in my name, and bills to pay.

I watched planes fly over the Hudson, and I envisioned getting onboard. I wanted more newness; I wanted to keep traveling. But I couldn't. I had responsibilities I had signed myself up for—trying to take care of a dog as a busy young person, finding a real job, paying rent, starting a 401(k) (whatever that was). College life and travels were in the rearview mirror. I would remain fenced in on this crazy island of Manhattan with the dog that people mistook for Cujo or Godzilla no matter how badly I wanted to escape it. But, for a girl, having a big dog people called Cujo had some advantages. Maybe we could still *kind of* escape.

It started with Central Park at night, a place I never would have considered going without my dinosaur at my side. We bolted up Eighth Avenue while patrons at bars and restaurants looked out at us like we were the cast of *Madagascar* escaping the zoo. The dollar pizza guys stopped with dough in hand, the customers at Shake Shack stared out the glass, a wave of heads turning in unison as the NYC misfits flew by. We darted through the herd of after-work traffic, faster than everyone, barging through business suits as people dove out of the way. We were on a mission: to leave the world of concrete and skyscrapers behind.

When we passed through Columbus Circle and reached the trees, I would look at Gizelle and say, just as I used to in college, "You ready? We're here! There's grass! Look at the grass!" I'd unhook her leash, and we'd disappear into the park. My feet softly swished against the grass and Gizelle's paws dug in to make a careening turn. And even though it wasn't Smoky Mountain silent, when I listened to our feet and paws against the earth, I felt relaxed.

We jogged through the trees, onto the sidewalk, and sometimes we'd cruise all the way to the Literary Walk, where I'd stroll with my head propped toward the bright sky. *I'm in Central Park! At night! With Gizelle!* I thought. That fact alone was worth every worry I had about my move to Manhattan. I felt so safe with my gentle giant in the park at night: she came up to my thighs, had a broad chest and a powerful, confident stride. Strangers would never know my dog with the head the size of a basketball was actually afraid of basketballs. Yet Gizelle did more than play bodyguard. I was twenty-three and had no idea what I was doing with my life. But when Gizelle and I ran through the park together, my fears disappeared. I knew I wouldn't ever be lonely as long as I had her.

During the day, Central Park belonged to millions of other New Yorkers, but at night it felt like ours. We walked to the grand tunnel by Bethesda Fountain. It was quiet and lit up in gold. Inside, we made all sorts of discoveries. Once it was a woman rehearsing Puccini in a long dress, and we sat on the ground to watch her for our own private opera show. Another night there was a violinist in a top hat who let us request all the songs. "Bob Dylan!" "Elvis!" "JT!" "*The Lion King*!"

I'd stroll home like a tourist with my head lifted toward the sky. Often we'd wind up at the New York Public Library by Bryant Park. The stairs were empty, and I would let out her lead so she could roam up and down, sniffing to her heart's delight until she'd finally find a place to sit with her bum backed into one stair, paws a step down. I'd sit next to her, with one arm around her, resting my head on her shoulder like she was a human, and this was a bench in our front yard, which in a way it kind of was.

But our favorite getaway of all didn't even require shoes or leaving the apartment building. At night, we'd sneak up five flights of stairs to the top of Rio. I'd kick open the broken door that said NOBODY ALLOWED ON ROOF, and step onto the roof. The fresh air would blast me in the face. Okay, the floor of the roof sloped into a slight U, it looked like someone may have patched it with duct tape, there were wires that seemed to serve no purpose, and when it rained there were puddles up there, but we had a view of the city lights. I'd put in my white earbuds and would warm up for ballet. And then because no one was watching (I hope), I'd pas de bourrée and leap and twirl across that roof like I was onstage at City Center. Gizelle would lie there and watch, her tail slapping the roof when I'd flick my toes and curtsey in her direction.

Up on the roof, no one was eyeing me, except for Gizelle. In fact, Gizelle would watch me like she had just spent her life earnings' worth of dog treats on a front row ticket to my show and it was an Oscar-worthy performance. Sometimes she looked at me like she loved me more than anything in the entire world. Sometimes she looked at me as though I were the entire world.

6

Working Girl

"This résumé looks perfect, Lauren."

There was no getting around it: New York was *expensive*. I had achieved the baseline requirement: I was a hostess, training to be a waitress. I cut corners like most young people in NYC: no cable, no eating out, no gym membership. I entertained myself by wandering around with my dog. But having a dog, especially a Gizelle-sized one, in New York City was a luxury in itself. Gizelle's grocery bills were more than mine, she was a frequent vet visitor with issues here and there—an eye infection, a UTI—and she required heartworm and flea and tick prevention, dog walkers, ear cleaning supplies, shots, and because she was bigger, her bills were always bigger. So, I utilized resources and pulled the "but . . . Gizelle is our family dog" card, and Mom and Dad helped pay for her, while I desperately searched for my first real job so I could chip in, too.

Like many eager young twentysomethings who move to New York City, I arrived in town with big dreams, little in the way of savings, and hardly any connections. I only knew that if I was going to get my bite out of the Big Apple, I was going to have to work for it. And even though I didn't have many leads on jobs and my employment "experiences" weren't deemed particularly important by anyone—internship at Dad's office, cashier at Cool Springs Mall slipper kiosk, waitress at Ruby Tuesday—I really wanted an office job where I could be creative and work on projects that I cared about. (I know—*Millennials*.)

My hostess gig was at a bar on the Upper West Side that served a confusing mix of sushi, fajitas, burgers, and pasta primavera. I got in the habit of coming home after a shift at Hi-Life Bar & Grill, showering, and crawling into bed. But instead of giving in to the urge of sweet, sweet sleep, I thought about how Dad kept telling me to "hang in there and keep working hard," and how Kimmy kept promising, "someone will hire you eventually." So, I would open my laptop, tuck my toes under Gizelle, and continue the search. I knew there was only one way to showcase Lauren as the best candidate for that great NYC job, my one and only chance at marching those heels I always borrowed from Kimmy into one of those shiny buildings in midtown. My golden ticket to a job somewhere in Manhattan: my résumé.

The nighttime honks of Times Square crept into the apartment. *Now, how am I going to make my life sound much more important than what it has been?* I mused, twiddling my fingers across the keyboard. Then I looked down at Gizelle laid out across my feet and tapped the bed, asking her to please come up here by me, and she did: maneuvering her body around to crawl up the bed until she was resting her nose on the edge of my computer. I sat for a moment, stroking her cheek and her silky ears. I knew exactly what I needed. Buzzwords. I needed buzzwords. Words like:

Excellent communication skills. Okay, this one was true. My best friend wasn't human, and yet I had just effectively communicated with her.

Problem solver. I did live in Manhattan with a dog the size of a Mini Cooper. You do the math.

Strategist and team player. Raising Gizelle required coordinating walks with Kimmy, and working with an array of free trustworthy babysitters.

Great public speaking skills. I'd presented in front of large groups of tourists in Times Square, delivering speeches like, "This is Gizelle, she is about a hundred and sixty pounds. Yes, that's around seventy-five kilos. Yes, her coat is called brindle. No, you may not ride her, sir. Yes, *English* mastiff. No, not a Cane Corso. No, not a Chihuahua, either. (Ha. Ha.) Yes, Photos are fine . . ."

Then I claimed to be proficient in Excel and Photoshop, organized and detail oriented, and with that, I set off, applying to nearly every entry-level job available in Manhattan in hopes of finding a career.

My dream was to be a travel journalist. I also wanted to start my own T-shirt company, charter my own big-dog nonprofit, and open a restaurant called Carbs You Dip in Stuff. But, I didn't know how one did any of those things. I did know how much my rent was. So, for the time being I lowered my expectations and focused in on finding stable employment, something with growth opportunities, even though sometimes I was terrified of what I would grow into. Often I didn't think I was anything but the talentless, scatterbrained, indecisive middle child who wanted to be too many things at once. I was a confused girl terrified of growing up, wishing she could hop around forever and never settle down.

But I tucked those fears away and set my mind on a career the way Gizelle sets her mind on a slice of dollar pizza, if one happens to be in my hand. She stares up at it with both desperation and determination, as though if she looked at it long enough, she could will it to miraculously become hers. I wanted one of those vital, consuming, high-profile jobs in Manhattan with free San Pellegrino in the kitchen and candy in the reception area, a mailroom, a security check-in, a badge with my photo on it, and a view of the Empire State Building. *I* wanted to wear a pencil skirt! And I wasn't giving up; I wasn't looking away, not even for a second, until I got it.

I must admit, looking for a career on my time off from the restaurant job was not so bad. I could spend the whole day with Gizelle. Sometimes we'd take breaks and stroll to Central Park on a Tuesday afternoon. I could bring my laptop to Bryant Park and apply to jobs underneath the canopy of trees with my mastiff at my feet.

I just kept sending out that résumé. And my résumé scored me some work. I earned a freelance gig writing about dishwashers and car tires, then a spot with a temp agency filing documents written in what seemed like hieroglyphics. The week after that I assisted a high-profile entertainment lawyer in the West Village who turned to stare at me when I answered the phone, and asked if that was my "real voice." (I still have my mom's high voice, by the way.) I temped in showrooms in SoHo and reception desks in midtown. I went on dozens of interviews and was constantly rejected. *No one is ever going to take me seriously with this damn voice.* I also applied to all the writing jobs on Craigslist that I could find, but it seemed as though neither my pen, my personality, nor any of the other tools I'd depended on thus far were going to land me a career.

I was beginning to feel like a nobody. But I still felt desperate to keep busy and productive, making use of every moment. So every time I went out with Kimmy and drank too much and slept away a Saturday, I felt guilty. But every time I stayed in, I felt guilty for not embracing New York City nightlife in my twenties. I couldn't win. All I wanted was to live in my own present moment and believe that I was exactly where I was supposed to be, but most of the time I only worried about all of the places that I wasn't.

A visit with Gizelle to Central Park at night was always a welcome break. When we passed through Columbus Circle and reached the trees, I unhooked her leash and always felt as though we'd jumped a fence and broken free. I watched Gizelle take off and I would chase after her, darting in between the lampposts and into the trees, with the city noise fading into the distance.

I never wanted to overdo the running with her but I still wanted exercise, so I created a "Mastiff Run," a workout regimen where I ran lifting my knees high, practically in place, while Gizelle strolled beside me, with no pressure to keep up. This running style would not win many points for exercise form, but it was great for nighttime in the park when no one was watching.

Sometimes we *ran* ran. Fast. "Go, girl, go! Run! Run! Run!" I'd yell to Gizelle, as our feet sprinted across the grass near Fifty-Ninth Street. When I ran, I felt strong and life felt simple. There were no decisions to be made; the only thing I had to do was put one foot in front of the other and not look back. When I ran, it was easy to stay focused on one thing. So to keep that focus, I kept making lists in an attempt to try to organize the life in front of me.

One night after many lists, many résumés, and a couple months of interviewing and temping and trying to "hang in there," I was sitting on the futon with Gizelle assessing more job opportunities, (aka stalking people on Instagram who had jobs and were a hundred times better at life than I was), when an email appeared in my inbox from Derek, Fashion PR Director. I had temped in his office and had been in for an interview a couple of weeks before.

"Kimmy!" I squealed. She was in the shower. *"Kimmy!"* I yelled louder, jumping from the futon with my laptop in hand to barge into the steaming bathroom as Gizelle followed, also trying to nose her way into the bathroom. I swung open the shower curtain.

"Kimmy!"

"Yeah?" she asked as she wiped soap from her eyes, unsurprised I would interrupt the middle of her shower. Nothing ever fazed her.

"Kimmy! I got a job!"

"You got a job?" Her face lit up.

"Yes, a job! A real job!"

She turned off the water, jumped out, wrapped herself in a towel, and gave me a bunch of high-fives, exciting Gizelle, whose tail knocked against the doorway while she licked the water on the floor, still trying to ease her way into the bathroom. "Tell me! Tell me! What's the job?"

My first job was in the office I'd imagined. Minimally furnished, with modern white lighting, concrete floors, and white trim and racks of clothes strewn across sleek hallways. There were big windows looking south at the Freedom Tower and north over Tribeca toward the rest of Manhattan. The place even had a cafeteria with affordable kale and grilled cheese! I had my own title and email signature.

Lauren Fern Watt

Gap Public Relations

PR Assistant, North America, Fashion PR

55 Thomas Street, 14th Floor

My first official job, and it was at Gap Corporate, the clothing company known the world over. The first day I arrived, I got a badge with my photo on it. *Check!* I rode up the elevator that was complete with a TV. *Check!* I looked out at the Empire State Building, and during a photo shoot, steamed a rack of clothes while listening to hip-hop music. *Check!* Then I was led to my office. There was a sign next to the door. I hoped it might say: LAUREN FERN WATT, PR ASSISTANT. But, it did not. It said: STORAGE CLOSET.

I did not mind working in a closet. It was a huge closet, filled with boxes and racks of clothes, and it had a desk with an outdated Dell laptop and a bulletin board where I hung a photo of Gizelle. The closet even had one window that faced another building's brick wall, which is like New York City's version of a stained glass window, if you ask me. There were mountains of shoes and multiple rolling racks stuffed with chambray, parkas, chunky knit sweaters, and vests, in no particular order. The place was a mess, as if a Black Friday shopper had turned a Gap Outlet upside down and dumped the contents into this one room.

My boss, Derek, was born to work in Fashion PR. He would strut in and out of the closet in his 1969 denim jacket with a crew of stylists and editors pulling pleather cross-body handbags for a 50 Under $50 Holiday Gifts story, or flannels for a Back-to-School Plaid story. Mostly they didn't need much from me, which left me feeling somewhat unimportant. But maybe it was worse when they did want something from me. Every time Derek asked for something, my cheeks warmed and I began blurting out nonsense phrases: "Yes! The academy blazer! GQ! Uhhh . . . maybe! The iconic G patchwork navy bomber?"

It didn't take long to discover that the main point of my job was to figure out new and innovative ways to fit and unpack eighty-seven large boxes of denim into a closet that was already filled with eighty-seven large boxes of denim, a task that sometimes reminded me of Gizelle, when she would attempt to fit into our dinky, compact bathroom in the morning to join Kimmy and me, who were already squeezed in shoulder to shoulder. She'd ease her way in behind our legs, pressing us into the sink with her head resting on the edge of the tub while Kimmy and I shared the mirror, a blow dryer on the toilet, mascara in the sink, scrambling over a dog the size of a Shetland pony to get out the door. It was impressive, really. Gizelle always had a knack for finding ways to fit in extraordinarily small places. And as I sat in my closet at work, buried beneath boxes of denim, I wished Gizelle could come and show me how to organize the boxes using her make-things-that-don't-fit-fit skill.

I wasn't a natural at closet organization, and it was almost as if the Big Apple were saying, *Oh, you wanted to work hard, did you? You wanted to climb the big corporate ladder? Well. Can you climb your way out of these boxes first?* Most days there were so many to unpack, I'd resort to shoving a few unopened ones to the back of the closet and switching the labeling so the new samples looked like old. Often I left work with my head down, feeling like a no one, wishing I knew what I was doing in life, wishing I were doing something with more purpose.

Juggling dog responsibilities with a nine-to-five job was another challenge. Every night I was all *okay, I'm going to wake up super early, walk Gizelle to off-leash hours in Central Park, read, write, meditate or something, and actually do my hair before work.* But then tomorrow would come and I would wake up to Kimmy throwing a pillow in my face and yelling at me from the doorway: "I already walked Gizelle. You're late!"

Other mornings I did wake up, my alarm still buzzing from the far-off corner of the room where I'd placed it so I'd *have* to get out of bed to switch it off, and my first thought was a state of denial. *Certainly I do not have to fit*

*in a morning walk before work. There is no way I have to
go out into the havoc of Times Square and pick up a massive,
steaming pile of poo in front of an audience, find something
to wear, hurry onto the packed A train to arrive at work by 9
a.m. What made me think this is what I wanted to do? Surely
this is a cruel joke.*

But Gizelle was mine, and my responsibility. Shirking
those walks, lingering too long in my bed, reminded me of
my mom. I was terrified of becoming my mom. I couldn't
even take naps or lie around watching TV without feeling immense guilt that I was lazy. So I tried to get better
at waking up with fewer snooze intervals to walk Gizelle
and get to work on time. Soon I realized that if Gizelle
and I did wake up early, we could run to Times Square at
6 a.m., when the streets were actually clear. The rising sun
bathed the whole place in a wash of pink. There were no
tossed Broadway-show brochures or trash, no cartoon characters or guys in green vests selling bus-tour tickets, just a
few street sweepers and smiling families huddled outside
of the *Good Morning America* offices clutching coffees. It
was magical.

The one factor that wasn't always magical was the rain.
If it was raining, Gizelle might very well decide she just
didn't feel like going that morning. We'd circle the block,
over and over. "C'mon, girl! Number two for Mommy!"
I coaxed. But Gizelle would stop and smell Every. Single.
Tree. I'd shake the leash. She'd pause for a second and I'd
get my hopes up, then she'd pull ahead to the next tree.
"Gizelle! I am late!" I'd warn, holding my wimpy broken

bodega umbrella over our heads that, in fact, did nothing to keep us dry. "Are all of these places unsuitable for you, girl?" I'd ask her. "Would you like me to plant you a rose-bush, princess?" Tree to tree she lingered until I'd give up. (*She was just going to have to hold that day.*) I'd hurry back to my apartment, rushing across Ninth Avenue with Gizelle in tow, trying to make it before the light turned. I watched the countdown on the crosswalk: 7, 6, 5, 4 . . .

"C'mon, Gizelle! Let's hurry, girl!"

And then, with no fair warning in the middle of Ninth Avenue, I felt a tug on the leash, looked behind me, and there was Gizelle with her back legs bent, looking at me, squatting.

3, 2, 1 . . .

HONNNNNNNK! HONK! HONK!

Besides fulfilling basic needs like getting in her walks, I worried about leaving Gizelle alone all day. Gizelle was very much a part of the everyday getting-ready routine, following me into the tiny bathroom, resting her muzzle on the ledge of the tub, or licking up the water on the floor. She always sat at my feet whenever I was in the kitchen, then she followed me back to my bedroom, watching me try on clothes, eventually making herself comfortable as she sprawled on the mountain of shirts I'd vetoed. Then she followed me to the door, where she couldn't follow me anymore. "'Bye, girl." I said sadly, as she gazed at me with her classic mastiff face, the one so desperate and sad I swore a tear might fall from her eye any minute. The face that made me feel like my heart was melting into goo. "I'm sorry you can't come, too."

She had a dog walker, as needed, and the vet reminded me mastiffs can sleep up to eighteen hours a day. Kimmy always walked her, too, sometimes coming home on her lunch break. Plus, the vet said Gizelle would probably be pretty content hanging out on the futon while I was at work. But still. I gave her extra water, food, set out all of her toys in front of her on the couch before I left, trying to put the red rope toy in her mouth because that one was her favorite. Sometimes Kimmy and I turned The Beach Boys on for her, or classical, even Italian lessons for a while, then I'd rush to the subway, hop on the A train to Tribeca, ride the elevator up, sprint to my storage closet, and keep making mistakes.

I sent editors blazers when I meant to send parkas, lost important sneaker samples, and pestered Derek with questions I should have known the answer to. I emailed Kimmy my Excel charts asking for help (*Why* did I say I was proficient at Excel?). Memorable was the day we realized we had no size 4 Boyfriend Shorts for our #Lifeisshorts Event *that* night, so I was directed to trek to every single Gap store in Manhattan to collect every pair of size 4 shorts in the bleached sexy luna wash I could find. "Get as many as you can!" my boss emailed. I came up with ninety of them, rewarded myself with an expensed cab ride back, and quickly received an email that said "*90?!* The budget!"

"Hang in there, buddy! You can do it!" Dad's voice always echoed in my head. My mom helped a lot then, too.

"Do you need a haircut sweetie? Can you afford a haircut? Let me treat you to a haircut!" and "No, no, no, your boss doesn't want to kill you. Just make sure you are still doing things that make Lauren happy. So proud of you, honey." I kept going.

After enough mistakes, I realized I wasn't such a disaster. I was great at smiling on cue, I learned to utilize resources and say the things people wanted to hear, and my work ethic helped the organizing boxes part get easier. But I often wondered if PR was for me. I watched the editors who came rushing in and out of my closet. They seemed so enormously crucial to what made New York City great. I tried to be grateful for having work, but between the Big Apple and the company job with all these cool, trendy, important people, it made the girl in the closet feel small. I wondered what Gizelle and I were doing in this city. It was clear: Gizelle was too big. I was too small. The only thing I did know was that if I wanted to venture up the corporate ladder that everyone kept talking about, I would need to stay in this closet for at least a year. *Good-bye, adventures,* I thought. I would never travel again, not on this salary, not with these hours. I wasn't going anywhere but home to Times Square, the Crossroads of the World, from one iconic global brand of a *G* to another iconic *G* that belonged entirely to me.

Thankfully, Gizelle was always a reminder that as self-centered as New York seemed to make you think you needed to be, I wasn't the only thing that mattered, and my closet job wasn't my only purpose. Gizelle didn't care if I unpacked boxes of denim for a living. Every time I walked in the front door, she'd jump from the futon (well, not "jump," first her front paws, then slooooowly her back end), then she'd wag and shake with uncontainable joy, her paws tapping against the wood floor. Gizelle helped me stop thinking about myself and my job and just feed my dog because she needed to be fed.

Then Kimmy would arrive home. "Wanna wash the pup tonight, Pook?" she'd often ask on the warmer days, opening up a bottle of Two Buck Chuck after her own long day at an internet startup. I'd look down at Gizelle, whose adventures on the streets of New York City always left her less than daisy fresh, and think, *We probably should.* We'd don our rattiest old shorts and fill our coffeepot, teakettle, and blender jar with warm water from the sink, and the three of us would troop to the back patio of Rio. We'd blast "Splish Splash I Was Takin' a Bath" and dance and suds up Gizelle, who never minded baths and stood patiently while we cleaned her. Unless we got so into our music that we neglected the bath altogether and climbed on top of Swamp Thang, swinging the towels over our heads and dancing. In which case Gizelle took the opportunity to shake before we were quite finished. "Shake it, Gizelle! Shake it, girl!" we'd yell, ducking for cover as water sprayed from her fur like a sprinkler.

The relief I felt coming home to Kimmy and Gizelle got me thinking . . . maybe the point of my closet job was to help me pay for the more important jobs. My job to wash Gizelle and laugh at how silly she looked when the water dripped over her head. My job to dance around the patio with my best friends, and dry Gizelle with a warm towel and then snuggle her tight when she was clean and smelled of dog and soap. I had to consciously remind the girl in the closet not to forget about my job of living and laughing and loving outside of the closet. Maybe there is a reason people stencil those cheesy words in their houses? Even if I sucked at my job and was a total New York City nobody, that didn't mean that I had to suck at everything else, too. Perhaps I could even make myself a human résumé. Maybe I wouldn't even have to lie: *Lauren Fern Watt: Totally disorganized. Doesn't know what she is doing but trying to remain positive. Excellent Live, Laugh, Lover.*

7

Meet a Boy

"Table for three?"

A friend of mine once told me that you just know you've made it in Manhattan when you have a job, a dog, an apartment, and a boyfriend. If that was the standard, I was three for four.

So: boys. Kimmy and I ventured to bars around the neighborhood searching for them, but all we found were finance guys married to their careers, tourists, cute boys holding hands with other cute boys, and more girls like us, looking for boys. The Gap office didn't provide many male options interested in me, and there were attractive guys on the sidewalks, but they all walked so fast.

The one time Kimmy and I did find cute boys was around Halloween, right when we'd arrived in New York City. We had walked into a bar on the Upper West Side called The Dead Poet dressed as matching panda bears. There standing in the doorway, like a match made at the zoo, were two tall, successful, male polar bears. It was fate! Next thing I knew (after a few too many shots of Jack) the four bears were piling into a taxi to drive downtown to Rio. The polar bear left before I woke up, I forgot his name, and he didn't leave a number. But he did leave a note on the Etch A Sketch on my door that said: "Thx." Was being a single girl in New York always this harsh?

I had come to the city to find myself—not a boyfriend—and I was usually content exploring the city with Gizelle. I liked my independence, and it was important to me to be the type of girl who didn't rely on other people, especially boys, for my own happiness. But as the days wore on, I couldn't help but realize that in a city of eight million people, I was beginning to feel a tad lonely. In a city of eight million people, I didn't know that many people. And even though I was proud of the fact that I wasn't afraid to do things alone and always had Gizelle and didn't *need* a boyfriend, I was still a Disney fairy-tale-loving loser. I wanted to believe someday I'd fall head over heels in love with a boy, and he would love me, too, and we'd teach each other things, and laugh together, and life without him would be unimaginable. (But . . . I would never admit that to anyone.)

Hey, a girl can dream, can't she? But a girl can also get real. If New York had taught me anything it was how to be efficient. I was quickly tiring of the bar scene, and it was expensive. So it only made sense that I should stop dreaming, stop complaining, stop telling myself that online dating was for desperate people and take advantage of one of the tools those smart Silicon Valley cupids invented to help us humans out: Tinder.

The first step in creating a Tinder profile is choosing a profile picture, and the last step in creating a Tinder profile is, also, choosing a profile picture. Tinder doesn't fake its priorities. Other than a small white text box at the bottom that you can fill with a tweet's worth of self-description/self-annihilation, all you have to do is upload a couple of photos. They can even be selfies. It's very simple.

One Thursday night Kimmy and I dove in. Lounging with Gizelle on the futon in our sweats, we buried our noses in our phones. "Runner, world traveler, PR girl from Nashville. Lives in Manhattan with really big dog." I typed, uploading a shameless, eye-catching selfie of me and Gizelle, figuring if a guy couldn't get on board with a really big dog, it would be best to get him out of the way immediately. I waved my Tinder profile masterpiece in front of Kimmy's face for her approval as Gizelle nestled her head in my lap, stretching out her legs and isolating me and Kimmy even farther into the corners until we propped our feet on top of her. "Yeah, yeah, sure! Looks perfect," Kimmy approved, barely even glancing because she was already off in Tinder land, rapidly running her finger across the phone. I set off, too, skeptically swiping through every boy claiming to be single within a twenty-five-mile radius of Rio.

Brooks, twenty-five, posing with a caged tiger? Nah, I much preferred the look-alike tiger whose snout was buried here in my lap.

Fist-pumping Kevin with lips pressed to a bottle of Grey Goose? Probably not the type who would jump out of bed to walk Gizelle if I pushed the snooze button all morning. Plus, I'm more of a bourbon girl.

Nick, with no face? Okay, your abs are nice, but do you have a head attached to that torso?

Cat-kissing Matt?

I mean . . . I love all animals . . . but I'll always be a must-love-dogs girl.

I swiped right on a lot of boys with dogs. They were low-hanging fruit. And when it seemed there was no hope for me, it was fun to Tinder for Gizelle, too, imagining what she might look like walking next to another profile dog in the park. *Left. Left. Left. Right. Left.* I swiped, laughing, poking Kimmy with my foot to show her guys I deemed especially ridiculous, snickering like a little girl at the boys who battled onscreen for attention. As I did this, Gizelle would emit a series of regular and profound sighs. She was silent on her inhales, but the exhales were deep and dramatic Chewbacca-like moans. If she could roll her eyes at me, this is how she would do it. I gave her head a soft pat, kept swiping and then . . .

"It's a Match!" The words danced across my screen with all the elegance of a PowerPoint animation. I tried to remember which one "Conner, 27," was. There had been no dog screaming out from the profile, but this didn't rule him out. I leaned in closer to my phone to explore. We had matching bungee jumping pictures, and unless he was being wildly deceptive with Photoshop, he also appeared to have hiked Machu Picchu.

When my profile picture, the one of me and Gizelle, lined up next to Conner's, the three of us lit up the screen. We looked cute on that screen. A couple of seconds later, he was writing me.

"Nice dog," he wrote. "What's your dog's name?"

"Gizelle."

"That's a great name."

And just like that, my first Tinder connection.

We exchanged phone numbers and started texting. I sent him the photo of Gizelle on my Times Square rooftop, and he sent me a picture of a pit bull mutt named Wolverine he'd lived with in college. Wolverine was wearing a Michigan sweatshirt. This was followed by another picture of his parents' dogs, three black-and-white fluffy papillons with underbites, also in Michigan getup. This was going so well! But then he sent one more picture of some fancy bottle of wine in a first class airport lounge. He added that he had bumped into George Clooney there. This felt a little boastful to me, but whatever. Conner had played football in college, studied for a year in Sydney, worked at a growing tech startup, and was training to be a sommelier on the side, just for fun. We decided to meet.

It was spring in Bryant Park. The winter ice-skating pond had been melted and stored away, the big green lawn was back to serve as a lunch table for nature-deprived business-people and their Chop't salads. Pigeons bobbed their heads and bathed in the fountains, pink tulips sprouted from big cement pots, the horses on the carousel spun round and round to the sound of French cabaret.

I showed up twelve minutes late and there he was, sit-ting with his ankle crossed over his knee beyond a group of black-suited finance types crowded around the bar of the Bryant Park Grill patio. He sat under a big green umbrella shaded under an even bigger umbrella of trees, BlackBerry in hand, waiting for me.

I felt as though the park pigeons had relocated to my stomach. I walked toward him, keeping my head down, praying he would recognize me so that I didn't have to be entirely responsible for the approach. I glanced at my phone, hoping I'd seem in demand and busy when in truth

I could count on the fingers of one hand the people who might be texting me.

I felt Conner looking at me and my cheeks began to burn. I forced myself to lift my head and our eyes met. He smiled, stood. No going back now. I slid my phone into my jacket and did a half wave of recognition as he got up and we slowly approached each other. He was taller than I'd imagined, wearing a light-blue button-down shirt that showed off a broad chest. For a moment I wondered if I had checked my hair after a cuddle with Gizelle before I'd left Rio. I ran my hands through my blond tangles and pushed the pony to one shoulder while leaving the opposite one exposed in what I hoped was an enticing way. *Remember, Lauren. You are cool. Just be yourself. Oh, but lower your voice. Yes, think Johansson sultry. You are Scarlett.*

"Hey!" I croaked, going in for a nonchalant one-arm hug. *Shit. Too high, Lauren, too high. Lower your voice, lower it.* "So nice to finally meet you!" I yelled out. *No! Overly enthusiastic. Scarlett would never say it that way.* Later Conner would tell me that he was surprised my voice was, well, what it is. Though I think he used the word "startled."

Conner was cuter than I'd anticipated. He had the broad shoulders of the linebacker he'd been, big football player hands to match, a short brown Chandler Bing cut, and straight-cut slacks. (I was head-to-toe Gap, hoping it somehow looked like Rag & Bone.)

We organized ourselves at the table and ordered two gin and tonics. Conner leaned back in his chair and I crossed my legs, putting one knee over the other, posing my hands in my lap. "Nice to do this. Work's been nuts," Conner said, as a short silence followed that I filled by smiling and nodding encouragingly. Then I quickly issued a disclaimer, saying how this was my first Tinder meetup and that I never did things like this but was new to the city. Although, I apparently *was* the type of person who did this; here I was doing it. For some reason the image of Gizelle finally giving in on her walk with Kimmy came to mind. She'd always seen herself as someone who pooped on grass, but in an instant she'd grown desperate and turned into the kind of dog who went on pavement.

The drinks sparkled in the sun. Conner listened to me ramble about the two G's in my life—Gizelle and the Gap. I did notice he said yeah a lot, quickly, even before I finished my sentences. Maybe he knew what I was going to say next and already agreed? Maybe he was nervous on this first date and didn't know what to say? Then he took his turn and talked about the class he was taking in oenology, the study of wine, and how he spent the weekends going to Chelsea Market, collecting spices he would then divide into jars and spend a great deal of time sniffing, which would improve his blind-testing ability. He even made flashcards to quiz himself. "It's fun," he told me. I looked at him, nodding my head *oh, tell me more,* but wondering if "fun" was the right word to use when discussing sticking your nose in a cup to smell oregano.

We sipped the sparkles from our glasses, and just as I

could feel myself drifting off, staring at the tulips in the park that were peculiarly shaped as stemware, Conner mentioned that he missed camping and hiking and was about to go to India for his friend's wedding. I'd been to India once and loved it so much, and I missed camping and hiking, too! I still wasn't sure about him, but I was willing to learn more. And just as I was mustering up the words, *You want to order another round?* Conner looked at his watch. "I actually gotta run. I have a client dinner."

Even though I wasn't wearing a watch myself, I knew our date hadn't lasted more than forty minutes. *Was it me?* I thought, embarrassed that I even cared.

"Oh, that's fine," I said, trying to brush it off. "I need to go walk Gizelle, anyway."

And he left, another one-arm hug good-bye, and I was left standing on the corner of Forty-Third and Fifth Avenue, confused.

I called Kimmy to let her know I was still alive, and she suggested a girls' Shake Shack night on the back patio of Rio. Gizelle and I climbed on Swamp Thang. Kimmy held forth in the chair across from us. "This guy sounds like a douche," Kimmy assured with her mouth totally full as she smeared a crinkle-cut fry into one of the dozens of ketchup containers. Sure, Conner had left fast, he seemed to take himself pretty seriously (judging from his hair gelled to his head and all of those flashcards), and I wasn't entirely sure he'd smiled or laughed once the whole forty minutes we were talking, but didn't "douche" seem harsh? Wasn't that the typical best-girlfriend response? If a guy doesn't like your friend, just call him a douche. He *has* to be a douche . . . But what if he wasn't a douche?

I handed Gizelle a fry, then leaned my head on her shoulder. As we sat on the back patio of Rio, which actually backed into a fluorescent-lit parking garage, I gazed down at the couch named Swamp Thang that had been snowed on all winter and now felt crunchy on my ass, and down at the week-old bottle of Charles Shaw I was drinking. I wasn't sure I'd end up dating Conner, the sports-obsessed wine guy, but I really wanted to meet new people. I wanted to try new things. I was curious. I was attracted to him. I wanted to see him again.

A few days later, Conner asked if I wanted to walk Gizelle and grab a bite to eat after work. I was always up for anything that involved food and Gizelle—Gizelle felt likewise. He arrived at Rio looking stylish in a slacks and sport-coat combo, but a little out of place in our apartment's kitchen/ living room filled with the eclectic mix of Ikea markdowns, sidewalk salvage furniture, and the Gizelle toys scattered about like a day care (the toys she never seemed to play with much). Gizelle introduced herself, as she did with most boys, first with a short, quiet bark, then once I said he was okay, she'd slowly approach with her neck out, gradually letting her tail out from between her legs. Conner did the whole "That's a big dog" routine, followed by a formal "It's nice to finally meet you, Gizelle." Then I ran around, Gizelle in tow, trying to locate keys-wallet-phone-combo while he thumbed at his BlackBerry and his iPhone went *bing!* in his slacks. We finally got to the door. "Ready?" I smiled, looping Gizelle's leash around my four fingers and propping the door open with my hip as she led us onto the street.

Gizelle walked calmly, casually shifting her weight from side to side, tail untucked, and I was thankful there weren't any scary buses within a close enough distance for her to crouch and run away from us on our first date.

As we strolled up Ninth Avenue, Conner suggested I pick the place because it was my neighborhood. This was bad news for me because Kimmy and I only ate dollar pizza and Trader Joe's, and sometimes, if we were really living large, Maoz Vegetarian, a do-it yourself falafel chain that Kimmy and I loved because you could get unlimited toppings and condiments. We also enjoyed going to Pinkberry, not to buy anything, of course, just to ask for samples and then step out fast like something important had come up. I wasn't about to suggest those dining experiences to Conner. So we kept walking up Ninth and I waited for the first decent-looking patio I could find, "This place." I pointed confidently, with no idea what *this place* was.

As Conner and I sipped extra-sour margaritas, Gizelle slurped water from an aluminum to-go pan. She made great first-date company, as any awkward silence could be quickly covered by turning the conversation over to her: "Gizelle, you okay? How's your drink, girl? More chips?" And then we could thoughtfully admire her stripes shining in the last bit of daylight or talk about the interesting comments about the mastiff from passersby, which helped to ease first-date tensions. On this evening, Gizelle seemed to be drinking with more than her usual gusto, slurping extra loudly, lapping water all over the place right in front of Conner. (Was she even *trying* to get any water in her mouth?) I knew what she was doing, of course. She was obviously just making a big watery-slobbery mess to see what this new guy would say, to see if he could earn the mastiff stamp of approval. "She's really goin' at it, huh?" Conner observed, a half smile playing on his lips.

"Yeah, she had a really tough day at the office." I joked, a little pathetically.

As we walked home, Conner took my hand. It was nice to be hanging out with a guy. He seemed confident, intelligent, and he was good-looking. But did I laugh on this date? Did I feel any butterflies?

Every few steps, Gizelle would look back at me, perhaps making sure I was okay with this grown-up man holding my hand. I watched Gizelle, too, making sure she was still okay with Manhattan foot traffic. With Gizelle, it was never quite clear who was watching whom. We watched each other, making sure we were okay with what life sent our way. And strolling down Ninth Avenue, past Greek and Italian restaurants, Irish pubs, and sushi bars after a dinner that didn't involve pillaging condiments and yogurt samples, life had sent us a grown-up I would eventually call my boyfriend.

First you're sitting four feet apart at a table in Bryant Park trying to sound interested in tannins and Tempranillo. Next you're bringing the dog camping in a lean-to at a lake, trying to forget that he told you s'mores were impractical and rolled his eyes when you asked him if he wanted to climb on top of the lean-to to look at the stars. So you look up at the sky by yourself, and swear this relationship doesn't feel quite right. But then when you get back to the city, he invites you to dinner at a restaurant so small it looks as if the whole place is eating together at one table. You eat beautiful food and sip delicious wine and have nice conversation, and even though you don't love the way he tends to review the restaurant like a critic and uses a multitude of adjectives when ordering wine, often calling the sommelier over to the table to ask him questions for which he seems to already know the answer, he still makes sure they boxed up leftovers for the dog. And when you leave, it's nice to have someone to walk home with. It's nice to have someone to slip into bed with. And in the morning you like the way he asks you to shower with him and you just stand there with each other, passing each other the shampoo with soap running down your noses, and it feels comfortable and normal, like you've been taking showers together forever. And deep down you believe he is a good person, and you like company and attention and having a guy around, so you keep seeing him.

Before long I was a regular at Conner's East Village apartment, thankful I had Kimmy to walk our fur daughter in the morning and noting that young single people should not have dogs unless they have nice roommates who also want dogs. Kimmy and I started hanging out less and less (never any drama, obviously; it was Kimmy, the easiest-going girl in the world). But her wild streak did not always mesh with Conner's more conservative nature. "Are you sure you like him, Fernie?" she'd always ask. "I see you with someone else." I'd tell her I didn't know, that this wasn't even a serious relationship. I was just having fun.

"He's fun?" she'd question. Soon she began going out with new friends of her own, and I liked that my new adult lifestyle didn't include downing water bottles filled with Smirnoff at electronic music festivals, not that there was ever much wrong with that. I just had my own set of issues with always trying to feel productive and grown up.

Conner was definitely a grown-up. He had a wine collection that was organized by region, varietal, and vineyard on a shelf designated for wine. His wine tools looked like instruments for surgery. He owned a rotating tie rack and two laundry hampers (one for lights and one for darks), and his closet contained clothes, on hangers, that he could actually find when he was looking for them. Everything on his wall was framed professionally: his college degree nailed into a corner, a painting of Prague, a big blue-and-yellow Michigan flag above his door. (Kimmy and I had a Zac Efron cardboard cutout in our window.) Conner was practical and organized. I lived in Times Square with a dog the size of a Mini Cooper. Perhaps practical would be good for me?

Conner did genuinely love my Mini Cooper. He was always talking to her, telling her how beautiful and silly she was, calling us "his ladies." He even paid to cab us places! Who cared if he didn't share my sense of humor and I found myself a bit quieter and more reserved in his presence? He brought Gizelle steak leftovers from Peter Luger! He taught me the mathematical strategy behind winning a game of Connect Four. I could call him for advice on how to deal with my boss and he'd send me an email right away with bullet points of advice. He seemed to know how to do everything, which was a relief, because I always felt like I was guessing.

I hadn't hung out in the East Village before Conner, but I liked it. It felt like a neighborhood. The people in the East Village looked like they actually lived in the East Village. There were not flocks of tourists in matching T-shirts following a leader holding up a flag on a ski pole, as there were around my place. There weren't sixteen Spidermen on every corner. Conner and I started Citi Biking together, then one weekend he left to go out of town for work and told me I should bike down to Avenue A and Ninth Street to check out the Tompkins Square Dog Run for Gizelle. "She would really love the dog run," he assured me. I biked downtown, over to Tenth Street between Avenues A and B, and when I saw the dogs running through the gravel park, splashing in a bone-shaped dog pool paradise under the towering trees, I knew Conner was right. Gizelle would love this dog run.

So I ignored the little voice inside that was terrified of

commitment, always telling me to bolt. I ignored the voice that kept telling me to leave because I didn't totally feel like myself when I was around him. I thought maybe if I hung around Conner long enough, I *would* feel like myself. And since I knew he adored Gizelle, I decided to believe he adored me as well and chose to ignore the fact that he never could find a way to say it to me.

8

The Dog Park

Tompkins Square Halloween Dog Parade

Soon it was my first official summer in NYC. As my relationship with Conner developed, I could feel myself outgrowing life in my Times Square apartment. The bustle and the chaos seemed louder. The streets got stuffier. It was too hot for Gizelle to walk far, so I was confined to midtown with her. Somedays I wondered if the taxis installed amplifiers on their horns, or if the lights of Times Square were broiling me like some sort of insidious tanning bed. Gizelle was shooed away from shady restaurant patios, outed from the Duane Reade freezer section where I tried to cool off, and turned away from taxis. My siblings were living the dream in California, seeming to excel at everything artistically and always texting photos from the beach. I was working a dead-end closet job, neighbors with the Times Scare zombies, drinking way too much at The Governor's Ball with Kimmy, and once a week Gizelle and I got asked out by a guy dressed as Cookie Monster.

Conner was out of town for work a lot. I was definitely *in* a relationship with him, but I couldn't quite seem to admit that to myself. Once I even quickly broke up with him, feeling trapped into something that was starting to look like a commitment, but I called him back and apologized, unable to figure out why I would end things in the first place. I was twenty-four and questioning everything. *Why did I move to New York? Is Conner a reason to stick around? Will I ever get a promotion at the Gap? Do I even want a promotion at the Gap? What am I doing with my life again?*

One evening I called my mother around nine, hoping she might convince me everything was fine and I was doing great in life, like she usually did. But that night she didn't pick up when I called. She didn't call me back.

A couple days later I called again. It rang and rang and when she picked up, she sounded as though she had just woken up. I asked her what she was doing. "I'm on my way to an eleven a.m. meeting."

"But it's eight p.m. your time." I pointed out. The phone went silent for a minute and then she guffawed.

"It's not eight p.m.!"

I paused for a second, looking at the clock on the microwave. It was definitely eight p.m. in Nashville. Then she carried on about a meeting with her friends Wendy and Craig and being sober and "better than ever," but as her words slurred into one another, it became increasingly difficult to make any sense out of them.

"Whatever, Mom. You sound drunk. I gotta run; I need to walk Gizelle." And just as she was trying to convince me she was only talking funny because she had Crest Whitestrips on, I hung up the phone.

Next came the bizarre texts. "Good morning!!! Baking fresh swirl and eggs today! Meeting at 3pm ddddddjjkkkkkkk." followed by rows and rows of colorful (yet inexplicable) emojis that I knew were not the result of bad iPhone skills.

Mom had lots of ups along with her downs, and it was impossible to keep track. Sometimes I'd call and she'd sound great. She was alert and she'd casually ask me questions about my day and if there was anything she could do to help me out in New York. I never knew which version of her I was going to get and each version tugged on my emotions differently. The sober (sounding) version gave me hope she'd be okay, and the drunk version crushed that hope. So my hopes were lifted and then let down over and over and over again. I didn't know how much more I could take. She would not even acknowledge she had a problem.

Sometimes I called my dad, hoping he'd provide words of sympathy when it came to dealing with Mom, but he didn't always say tons about her. Often he said things like, "Well. Fernie. Ya taking care of yourself there, buddy? How's the job going?" And that was it. Then I'd get so mad that he wouldn't say the words *I* wanted to hear, which were: *"I'm so sorry. She'll be okay. You'll be okay. This will all be okay! Let's fix her! I'll fix her!"* that I'd hang up the phone on him, too.

Yet even on the most stagnant summer days in Hell's Kitchen, I could find a breeze on Rio's rooftop after the sunset. So I climbed to my rooftop with Gizelle. The lights of Times Square flickered around us. Gizelle sat at my feet, and I sat down in front of her with my legs crossed. Our eyes locked. We stared at each other, and I always marveled at the way she would hold my gaze. Peering out of the dark-black mask of her face, those curious, concerned, downturned eyes were always comforting. I thought about the inside of Gizelle's brain, how my sister once told me it was probably filled with nothing but a vast field of green with a single tulip growing in the middle. Then I thought about the inside of mine, which felt a lot like Times Square. Loud. Congested. Too many messages flashing at once.

All I wanted was to exist in the moment, on my rooftop with Gizelle. But I couldn't stop my mind from worrying. I worried about losing my mom and wondered how to fix her. I worried if Conner was the right person for me. I worried I was working the wrong job, how I would ever find the right job, and about not having friends in New York. Kimmy and I were slowly drifting apart, being pulled in different directions, and I could feel it happening but I didn't know what to do about it. When I'd first moved to New York City, I'd promised myself I would live a life of adventure, but now I was feeling stuck in an expensive city working a nine-to-five job and not having much of an adventure at all. I thought about leaving and where I might go. I could pack up with my trusty four-legged best friend, tape my insecurities into a box, and not have to unpack them again for months.

I threw my arms around Gizelle. She propped her big head over my shoulder, letting me lean all of my weight into her as the lights of midtown flashed around us. She was always my support whenever growing up became too confusing.

As the heat and summer wore on, I started dreaming more and more about our escape plan. And just as I started writing lists about where we would go next, I received a Facebook message from an old friend.

"Do you live in the city now? I just moved here on 46th and 11th! I want to meet Gizelle!" Rebecca wrote.

I knew Rebecca from College of Charleston freshman year. Rebecca was the girl who would drive to Folly Beach and jump in the ocean with me, no matter how cold the water was. She was from Boston, and her speech was occasionally scattered with the word "wicked." She loved poetry, healthy organic food and Nina Simone.

She was also a lists girl, like me. One of the first times we spoke was in her dorm on the fourth floor of the McConnell Residence Hall talking about how to stay focused in the requirement classes we had no interest in. She laughed.

"Want to hear something I wrote in statistics today?"

I nodded. "Sure." She pulled a ripped-up green spiral notebook from her desk and flipped past some notes until she landed on a page. Then she cleared her throat, jokingly. She went on to read me a weird and wonderful list of things she loved: sharing a planet with the octopuses, the way roses look after rain, black holes. Rebecca kept silly journals the way I did, writing everything down so life didn't get away without her documenting it. When I left Charleston, we'd promised we'd keep in touch, but didn't. We'd actually hardly spoken until one night in July, when she wrote me out of the blue about how she'd moved to Hell's Kitchen, coincidentally a couple of blocks away.

Gizelle and I met up with Rebecca on the corner of Forty-Third and Eighth. Rebecca was wearing old, beat-up brown boots and a white flowy dress. "Oh my god," she laughed, "Gizelle! You are beautiful, girl!" She clapped her hands and bent down as Gizelle walked right into her arms for a hug (Rebecca totally ignored the slobber Gizelle left on her dress). We jumped up and down and hugged each other. "I can't believe you live here!" Rebecca cheered. "I can't believe *you* live here!" I cheered right back. We hugged again on the sidewalk. Then she took Gizelle's leash like they were old pals. As we walked to Rebecca's apartment, the same old rude comments about the mastiff from passersby continued, but we didn't pay much attention. "Don't listen to them, Gizelle!" Rebecca assured. "You are *not* a big f'in' dog. You are a curvy, voluptuous, beautiful queen!"

Rebecca's apartment was a dusty, old, furnished sublet above a taxi repair shop and a pet spa. The place had cardboard walls, stacks and stacks of old books and instruments, an antique dentist's chair in the living room, plants hanging from the ceiling, and a beat-up Steinway right in the middle of it all. Her home was also no stranger to cockroaches. "I do ballet in the living room!" She beamed as she did a little twirl on her way to the kitchen to get Gizelle water.

And just like that, I knew we had another friend in the city.

Rebecca and I did everything together. We took Gizelle thrift shopping and bought matching floppy hats. (Yes, we bought Gizelle a hat, too. This was how we justified buying the third hat in blue.) We colored our lips dark red and set off to talk our way up to the Boom Boom Room, a glamorous, 007-type, gold-colored lounge with a 360-view of Manhattan. Undaunted by the line, Rebecca declared, "I got this," strutted to the front, and talked with the bouncer, asking him about his day, until we skipped right through the door. Did I mention she was drop-dead gorgeous? Curvy with golden-brown eyes and perfect skin and boobs. At any one time she had a multitude of guys swooning over her.

The more time we spent together, the more I saw something in Rebecca that reminded me of my mom from way back when: If I was uncertain, she built me up. When I worried, she soothed me and turned me around. Soon I realized I was calling Rebecca with a lot of the worries I used to call my mom with, and I tried not to pay attention to the fact that my actual mom hadn't called me in a few weeks. Rebecca would listen to me ramble about my problems until the end of the world if I needed. She always made me feel like everything was going to be okay, because somehow Rebecca had a way of always making everything okay.

Rebecca worked at a world-renowned ad agency as an account executive. "I have no idea how I got this job. I totally tricked someone," she smiled. She spent time working on side projects, writing a play or TV pilot. Later she would run a hot-sauce company called Itso Hot Sauce. Together we decided Gizelle should really start pulling her weight with her expenses, so we did what all the other pet owners of that time were doing: we made Gizelle an Instagram account. *She's going to be famous!* we hoped as we took over the username @GizelleNYC and the hashtag #BigDogBigCity. We journaled photo ideas, and even set up a photo shoot with balloons in the park. We planned to take her to every borough all over New York City and take pictures of her and that would eventually launch our next careers. But we only made it to four posts.

With Rebecca, New York began to look different to me. On my own, I felt like I was watching New York City go by from Rio's rooftop, but now I began feeling like I was a part of the city. I wasn't just surviving in it anymore.

The inevitable let's-take-this-to-the-next-level conversation came one night toward the end of August, at a table on the sidewalk of a tiny French bistro called Tartine in the West Village. The restaurant was tucked between brownstones and skinny streets with pretty names like Waverly and Charles and Perry. Streetlights lit the table. We were sharing mussels, fries, and a bottle of wine we'd brought. It came up that both of our leases were ending soon. I was telling Rebecca how I wasn't sure about staying in New York City, that it was so expensive and I missed my siblings. I confessed that I didn't know where I belonged or what I was doing, but I didn't want to be stuck in Times Scare for another year.

"Well. We could look for a place together?" Rebecca said slowly, opening up a mussel, the hesitation at the end of the sentence signaling that she knew I was unsure about it too.

"But do *you* want to live together?" I asked.

Rebecca looked at me curiously.

"Because you know that means living with Gizelle . . . "

"And Gizelle is a great roommate. But she can be a tad smelly. She slobbers, but I clean that right up. She also sheds, like, a lot. Sometimes I wonder how she actually still has fur *on* her. But it's fine because I have a big lint roller."

Rebecca smiled and nodded as I continued to ramble.

"And I mean, you've seen her poos. They are . . . well . . . you've seen them! But that's easy to get used to, just need extra gloves and bags and to always be prepared. And sometimes boys are kind of scared of her; she barks at them if she doesn't like them, but it's a great way to filter out the guys you probably shouldn't have around, anyway. Oh, and I definitely need help walking her, never would have made it this past year without Kimmy . . . " My voice trailed off as I reached for a mussel. I loved Kimmy, and she'd done so much for me and Gizelle, but something about moving in with someone new, getting a fresh start, felt right. Kimmy had even mentioned moving in with new friends in Brooklyn.

"Girl. I love Gizelle." Rebecca smiled.

"I'll totally help you."

Then she held up her glass of Cabernet (that according to Conner did not pair well with mussels, but we didn't care).

"Roommates?"

"Roommates."

One month later it was nearing the end of September and I packed up my room. Gizelle watched with the most concerned *where are you going?* face. I don't think she blinked once all day, following me eagerly from the living room to my bedroom as I packed up our life in midtown. "You're coming, too," I assured her over and over as her toenails clicked behind me. I stuffed Gap clothes in trash bags and laundry hampers, rolled up my big map of the world, and hauled Swamp Thang onto the sidewalk and left a sign on him that said FREE TO GOOD HOME.

Rebecca and I rented a U-haul pickup. I tossed my final trash bag into the bed of the truck and squished Gizelle's dog bed into the last bit of space. I turned around and took one final look at Rio. *Good-bye, Rio,* I thought, dropping my shoulders and letting out a sigh. I shut the tailgate of the truck, climbed over Gizelle (who'd apparently called shotgun) to take my spot in the middle seat. Rebecca put one hand on the wheel, stepped on the gas, and I gazed out at what would soon be my old neighborhood disappearing before my eyes. "So long, Times Square!" Rebecca yelled, turning up Whitney Houston on the radio.

Gizelle stuck her giant head out of the window, taking whatever last sights the sporadically moving truck could showcase in stop-and-go traffic, ducking her head back in the car whenever a bus roared by. And with Rebecca on my left and Gizelle on my right, I left the lights of midtown, Rio, the Times Scare, and my first year in Manhattan behind me, ready to begin another chapter in the really big city with my really big dog.

Our new home was on Seventh Street between Avenues A and B, and I could see the Tompkins Square Dog Run from the window. I couldn't wait to show Gizelle our new neighborhood. We sprinted down the stairs onto the sidewalk. The East Village air felt cool and new, and the sidewalks weren't swollen with people. There were kids laughing in the park on Ninth Street and birds chirping in the elm trees above the dog run. Church bells rang in the distance.

As we strolled up Avenue A, a woman in a black leather jacket approached. When she got closer, her mouth opened without making a sound. For a second I thought *here we go again*, expecting the pointing, the swearing, the photo ops, to all continue. But instead, she squinted her eyes, stuck her finger out at Gizelle, and said:

"Biscuit?"

That was one I hadn't heard before. Did she know we were from the south?

"Biscuit?" I questioned.

"Yeah, Biscuit. Isn't that Biscuit?" she asked, leaning her head toward Gizelle. "Oh, wait!" She smacked her palm to her head before I could say anything. "That's not Biscuit! I'm so sorry . . . it looks *just* like her." She laughed and told Gizelle she was beautiful and walked away.

A couple of minutes later a guy in a Jets T-shirt approached, studying Gizelle. I braced, waiting for it. I was ready for my response (*No you may not put a saddle on her!*). Instead, he stopped, looked at Gizelle, and said:

"Summer?"

This scenario with Summer and Biscuit kept happening. Then people kept telling me about this guy named Louie whom I just had to meet. "You will know him when you see him," they promised. "He has dogs just like Gizelle."

"He has like seven of them!" one lady called out.

Dogs like *Gizelle?* In New York *City?* Was this some urban legend?

Then one day I turned a corner to walk into Tompkins Square Park with Gizelle, and coming at us was none other than Louie and his two colossal, wrinkly, lion-headed mastiffs. One was fawn and one was brindle and the three of them together almost moved in slow motion, as though they were one creature. He had long, curly, scraggly hair, a Santa belly, and he wore a shirt that said "Drool is Cool." I found myself wanting to bow down to his greatness.

"This must be Gizelle," Louie cackled, as the three mastiffs met in the center of the park.

"It is!" I smiled, feeling honored he knew Gizelle's name. I looked down at Gizelle, who was touching noses with the other brindle girl, Biscuit, as their thick tails slowly swung behind them.

"They're the best dogs in the world, aren't they? Like humans." Louie beamed, patting Summer on the head. Her eyes closed contentedly with each pat just as Gizelle's always did. He told me he used to have five of them in his apartment on Ninth. I wasn't about to ask him how he fit five English mastiffs in his apartment, but I did agree with him on one thing: Gizelle was like a human.

It was clear just how human Gizelle was when we ventured into the Tompkins Square Dog Run for the first time. It was a Saturday, and just like everywhere else on weekends in Manhattan, there were crowds. This place seemed to be home to every breed imaginable—Pit bulls and Vizslas, toy poodles and corgis, mutts, Labs, Dalmatians, pugs, Great Danes, puppies, and now, beautiful brindle mastiffs.

"Ready, girl?" I asked, sliding open the black gate and un-hooking her leash.

A clique of three Labs bounded over to meet my girl. They scampered around her in circles, barking and taking turns attempting to shove their noses toward Gizelle's behind as she backed her rear away from them, ears pushed back on her head, tail tucked, almost offended. She scooted toward me, attempting to barge her rump between my legs, but the moment the dogs lost interest and ran to greet the next arrival, her tail untucked and she followed behind them curiously, as though she wanted to be friends but wasn't quite sure how.

She circled back to me. "I know, girl. There are a lot of dogs here; it's okay to be nervous," I assured her. I walked over to sit on a bench in a patch of sun and Gizelle followed behind, taking her place at my feet or, more precisely, on my feet. And this became her usual dog-park routine: me sitting on the bench in the sun watching the dogs, and Gizelle sitting devotedly with me, also watching the dogs.

Of course, there was a lot of action. One Jack Russell terrier was hell-bent on digging through the gravel as though he just knew that he'd buried his treasure trove of Milk-Bones somewhere in this park and couldn't figure out where. Rabbit, a sneaky beagle mix liked to steal articles of clothing—other dogs' sweaters and humans' scarves—and was delighted when the owner picked up on this game and chased him around the park. One Lab begged his dad to throw the tennis ball then, without fail, refused to give the ball back. There was a Boston terrier mix who loved eating his own number two (and other dogs' number twos). Nearly every owner in the park ran at him trying to stop the pup from succeeding, but that crap-eating terrier won every single time.

Gizelle never did those inherently doglike things. She never barked unnecessarily, howled into the night, or chewed the remote. She didn't hump her squirrel stuffed animal or go to town on anyone's leg (thank god). I never even saw her drink toilet water. (Though I may have turned a blind eye to the slobber on the seat on a few times.) She enjoyed sitting in a warm bathtub like a human. She yawned like a human, letting out a long, satisfied Chewbacca moan. And except for one incident with a stinky block of blue cheese Rebecca and I once left on the low coffee table, Gizelle never helped herself to snacks that weren't hers. In fact, I had become so accustomed to having a non-dog dog, that I once brought my coffee and bacon-egg-and-cheese bagel *into* the crowded Tompkins Square Dog Run on a busy Saturday morning, assuming I'd pleasantly sit on the bench with a book and enjoy it. This was a blonde moment, obviously.

The Tompkins Square Dog Run was a place for every breed imaginable, and there seemed to be every type of human imaginable, too. An elderly woman with a dinosaur stitched to her shirt had a brown shaggy mutt named Cookie. She had lived in this neighborhood for forty-five years, forgot me every time she saw me, but loved to retell the same stories about the grittiness of the East Village thirty years ago, before the yuppies had moved in. She told me she hated how all those young people moved to the East Village and pretended Manhattan was their home when they'd only lived there a year. I told her those people were the worst. Another man pulled his sweet pit bull with bad back legs in a red wagon to the park, just so the pup wouldn't miss out on the fresh air and fun. There was a gray Great Dane who was taller than Gizelle. He wore a John Deere collar and his owner wore a cowboy hat.

But the best day in the dog run, without a doubt, came toward the end of October. I woke up before my alarm (shocker) and shook Gizelle. She cranked one eye open and left the other squished into the pillow. I jumped out of bed, which was often the only way to get Gizelle out of bed. She climbed off the mattress, first scooting her front paws off the ledge, leaving the back half of her still resting while she paused for a moment to look at me, ruefully trying to figure out exactly why we were getting up at all.

Rebecca was in the living room at the record player, turning up one of the only albums we owned: Stevie Wonder's "For Once in My Life," which we deemed Gizelle's favorite song. I opened the windows, letting in the fall breeze as we climbed onto our fire escape to sip our morning coffee. It was the 23rd Annual Tompkins Square Halloween Dog Parade, the largest dog costume parade on the planet. And the contestants were already arriving.

We stood on the fire escape that looked over the park

and pointed out our favorites. Gizelle propped her chin on the window.

"I got a cast of *Star Wars*," Rebecca announced. "Leia, Chewy-Yorkie, Luke, a Stormtrooper-mutt, and, ah, a Yoda pug. That's gonna be a tough one to beat, G."

I took a deep breath. "Oh, I see, a—wait—is that a Pomeranian? With a pumpkin on its head coming out of a Starbucks cup? Is that a *pumpkin* spiced *Pomeranian?* Shit. We're screwed."

"God, I don't know, but that's Sharknado," Rebecca laughed. "No, sorry, it's Sharkna*dog.*" A curly black-and-white dog with a black tornado made of felt and toy plastic sharks wrapped around him. I gazed over the park, spotting two poodles dressed as Jack and Rose, thinking how Gizelle would have made a wonderful *Titanic.*

Rebecca went inside to mix Bloody Marys in the kitchen. "Cooking with Lauren and Rebecca," we joked, stirring fresh tomato juice with long sticks of celery and tossing in olives and Itso Hot Sauce. Then I began shredding a big white T-shirt (from Gap, of course), cutting holes in an effort to make it look like Gizelle had torn it to shreds herself. Then I tried to convince her to chew up some baseballs, but she wasn't going for it. She looked at them, tilting her head, unsure of what they were. So, with a little scissor and knife work, the baseballs took on a genuine chewed-by-slobbery-beast look. *Perfect.*

We were going as the crew from *The Sandlot*, the movie about a kids' baseball team in the '60s, complete with a mastiff known as The Beast rumored to have eaten children for trespassing on its turf. Rebecca and I threw on flannels and baseball hats. We colored name tags that said "Ham" and "Scotty Smalls" and set off into the park.

Tompkins Square was madness. The entire cast of *Cinderella* walked by. A cocker spaniel was wearing a blonde wig and a blue dress inside of a pumpkin carriage being pulled by a Lab dressed as a horse draped in sashes. The owners were dressed as prince and princess. I stepped to the side of Gizelle, shielding her view of the *Cinderella* foursome—no need to amp up any pre-runway jitters. Also, no need to remind Gizelle that they don't make princess carriages in her size. "You're the prettiest one here," I confirmed confidently, patting her on the head. There were Ghostbusters, dinosaurs, Beanie Babies, and even a Pope Francis. Gizelle was doing an excellent job remaining calm about the competition, so much so that she lay right down on the gravel.

A green Astroturf path served as a runway in the middle of the Tompkins Square Dog Run, and three judges sat at a table next to it. Some of the owners had prepared songs to sing as their dog strutted; some acted out skits. I squeezed Rebecca's hand. Shit. We didn't have a skit. Were we ready? We moved with the line, waiting for our turn, until finally we were next. I wrapped Gizelle's leash around my wrist. We climbed to the stage, a little wooden runway built in the middle of the dog run. Gizelle sat at my feet. This was it.

"And next," the announcer boomed.

The whole crowd was still. (Well, semi-still—only so

much to be expected from festive New Yorkers and their canine companions).

"The moment this English mastiff has been preparing for her entire life . . ." I took a breath.

"Taking the stage . . . we have *Gizelle* as The Beast from *The Sandlot!*"

I looked down at Gizelle.

"Okay. Walk."

I gave her leash a little wiggle and she strutted her muscular body down the runway, showing off her curves, a little smile this way, slight turn of the head. She performed the perfect open-mouth pant to entice the crowds; she worked up some slobber from her jowls, really getting into character. *Strut, strut, strut, turn, show a little Beast! You are mean. Fierce! Roar!*

We reached the end of the Astroturf, and the crowds *roared* for Gizelle.

"Again! Let her walk again!" they yelled. We got off the stage and I bent down to my girl, rubbed her ears, and kissed the spot in between her eyes above her nose. "You did it, girl! You're such a model! Most beautiful Beast ever!" For a moment I thought of my mom, who used to always tell us we were the standouts in our dance recitals even if we'd been stuck in the back row.

It's possible Gizelle hadn't really *strutted* that day; there's a chance she sat for a second in the middle of the runway and I had to kind of pull her. But she was the best one to me. She was even named number sixty-seven on Buzzfeed's list of The 70 Best Costumes At New York City's Most Important Dog Costume Competition! Talk about achievements! Was this the same dog that used to hide under the table from balloons? The dog that had run away from floating plastic bags? My beast had come a long way.

Later, after losing to some admittedly impressive chef Chihuahuas sitting next to big lobster pots, one of the announcers stopped me. "You guys totally should have won. Gizelle knows how to work a runway." I smiled, then I looked around the park. Looking out at all the different types of people and their different types of dogs on a beautiful fall day in Tompkins Square, I had a warm feeling inside of me. It was a feeling similar to the one I'd had when I'd first gotten Gizelle. A feeling of being attached, a feeling of being home.

Things with Conner had even been going well. Gizelle and I spent many fall evenings enjoying the walk to First Avenue to stay at his apartment, which was much nicer than ours. It had reliable climate control, food in the fridge, Apple TV, and a boy to cuddle with. He always made Gizelle a bed on the floor, and he usually had some sort of leftovers for me to eat. Then I'd dig through his organized closet, careful not to mess up anything (but usually failing) until I found my favorite T-shirt of his. I'd fall asleep wrapped in his arms and everything seemed okay.

But sometimes I'd jerk awake, and then I wouldn't be able to fall back asleep. I'd stare at the ceiling, look over at Gizelle snoring, look over at Conner snoring, listen to the faint sounds of traffic on First Avenue. I'd close my eyes hoping sleep would come. Nothing. Then after forty minutes or so I'd give up, creep out of bed, slip on my shoes, clip on Gizelle's leash, and walk back to my apartment at 4 a.m., thankful I had Cujo to keep me safe on the late walk home on Seventh Street. Then I'd get to my own bed, where I would snuggle with Gizelle and wonder why I'd left in the first place.

Soon December rolled around, and I didn't want to leave New York, but Conner agreed to baby-sit Gizelle when I went home to Tennessee for Christmas. So I kissed the two of them good-bye and took a bus from Grand Central Station to LaGuardia Airport. Dad picked me up at the airport in Nashville. We drove to Mom's apartment near Vanderbilt to meet up with Tripp, Jenna, and Erisy, who were just in from California. Usually, Mom's house at Christmas would look like the North Pole, but as I walked in the front door and looked around, there were no Christmas decorations. There was no Christmas tree.

Tripp, Jenna, and Erisy sat on the living room floor surrounded by a pile of crafts—felt, pipe cleaners, jingle bells, bows, red sweaters, and flannels. They were making outfits for a holiday party the following night. Bing Crosby was crooning from Tripp's iPhone, and *The Muppet Christmas Carol* was playing on the TV in front of them. Erisy jumped up and presented me with a beautiful plaid Christmas flannel she'd crafted. It matched the one she had made for herself and could have put Martha Stewart to shame. "Oh my god, this is so perfect—I love it!" I beamed as we hugged. (How is she so damn good at everything?) Dad carried my suitcase to the upstairs guest bedroom. I took off my coat and Erisy and I scurried into the bathroom by the kitchen to try our shirts on. Tripp and Jenna followed shortly after and all of us piled in the tiny bathroom to look at the Christmas creations. Just as I was asking Tripp if we should wear our sweaters to this old Nashville dive bar called the Villagers Tavern to play darts, we heard it.

A horrible scream followed by a heavy thud of a body dropping to the ground. We raced out of the bathroom and up the stairs to find Mom on the floor, with Dad bent on the ground holding her head up in his hand. "Call 9-1-1!" Dad shouted. Mom's whole body was stiff, her hands locked into claws and she was convulsing. We stood for a second, trying to fathom what was happening.

"Get HELP!" Dad yelled louder. "GET HELP FAST!" I had never seen my Dad so afraid. We jumped into action. Tripp ran to his phone to call 911. Jenna ran to get a pillow to support my Mom's head. I rushed out the door to a dark, quiet street in Hillsboro Village. The cold hit my face and my toes as I stood barefoot in my Christmas flannel. *Heeeeeellp!* I screamed, hearing the desperation in my own voice, not even knowing whom I was calling to. Erisy ran out after me, her scream far more high-pitched and angry, tears falling down her face. "She looks like she's dying! Is she dying? Is she *dying?*" Erisy cried. Before I could respond, she held her fists to her face and belted, "HEEEEELLLLP!" Her scream was worse than my Mom's. "HELP!" she cried again, as a few neighbors stepped out of their houses. I grabbed her hand, trying to pull her to me. Then we heard the siren.

By the time the paramedics arrived, Mom's convulsions had slowed down. She was semiconscious, breathing, but still on the floor, unable to speak. I stood on the stairs and watched the paramedics lift her from the ground and buckle her into an upright stretcher. Her head swayed off to the side, squishing her cheek against her shoulder. I rushed to grab shoes for her to have at the hospital and found the closet stuffed full of Target bags filled with glittery Christmas decorations, tags still attached. The mom I knew she wanted to be stuck right there in the closet.

I sat in the front seat of the ambulance and rode to the hospital. I don't know why it was me in the front seat, but somehow as the oldest daughter, I always ended up being there. The rest of my family followed in a car behind us. The driver asked me if Mom had a drug problem.

Yes.

Does she know it?

No.

Does she have a drinkin' problem, too?

Yeah.

Does she know she has a drinkin' problem?

I shook my head.

The holidays are hard on us all, he said. Then he told me he once loved an addict, too.

Mom stayed three nights in the hospital. On Christmas Eve, we drove to her apartment to say good-bye. We would stay in Tennessee for Christmas, but she was leaving for rehab again, this time in Florida. But I didn't care. I promised myself I didn't care even as I spent an entire day on the phone trying to locate the right rehab. I hugged Mom good-bye. Not tight. I didn't want to hold onto her anymore.

9

The Limp

A few weeks later I was back in New York City. Winter had its grip on the East Village—ice, snow, slush, heavy wind. There was no more back patio of Rio, and it was too cold to bathe Gizelle in the Tompkins Square Dog Run with the hose like I did in the early fall. So I bathed her in my bathtub, where she appeared to be so calm and serene that I sometimes considered lighting candles for her and opening a *Vogue*. Of course, when she got out of the tub and shook herself dry in the bathroom, splattering me and everything else with wet dog hair, the serenity quickly disappeared. But Gizelle liked the bath so much that occasionally she'd crawl in there to sleep when I wasn't home.

Once I was sitting in a bath, Gizelle was hanging out in the bathroom, drinking the bathwater as usual, until she put one paw up on the ledge. *She wouldn't, would she?* I thought, patting her head as her fur clung to my wet hand. She put a second paw up. *Nah, no way.* And then before I even had time to stop her, she dropped her front paws in the tub and heaved her backside over in an attempt to be smooth and graceful but cannonball splashed the water all over the tile. *Well, this is new, Gizelle,* I thought, tucking my legs to my chest as the water calmed and she sat panting happily, as though we did this together all the time. Gizelle sat, delighted with the chance to once again show off her mastiff superpower: making-things-that-don't-fit, fit. And also her other dog superpower: the *I'm always here for you, girl* one.

Back in New York, I had physically escaped my mom's

problems again, but this time the problem did not escape me. When I closed my eyes at night, I saw my mom being strapped into a stretcher, her lifeless head bobbing off to the side. I saw the color sucked out of her face, the blue under her eyes. I realized that I couldn't even remember the last time I'd seen her and been 100 percent sure she was sober. In my dark bedroom of the East Village, I realized all my memories of my mom were clouded with uncertainty. Had she been there the day she'd taken me to buy Gizelle? What about when she'd visited me in New York City? In my bed at night, I searched my memories for my mother's voice, her soft, high, lilting voice, not the one that sounded slurred and dazed. And I searched for her smile. But I couldn't find the memories anywhere. But when I thought about the Christmas decorations I'd seen in her closet, I held on to the fact that *that* was the mother she was and wanted to be.

But my mom was deep in denial. That was why I hadn't known what to tell the ambulance driver when he asked me if she knew she had problems. Sometimes it was easier to believe she was fine than accept the truth that she wasn't. Sometimes I had conversations on the phone with her when she was totally drunk just because I missed her and wanted to talk to her, and I couldn't ever decide what was worse: to have her in my life with her addiction or not have her in my life at all. But I didn't want to live in denial anymore. Denial was holding my mother hostage. So I attempted to move on and cut my mother out of my life.

Dad suggested I get more involved in Al-Anon, a support program for friends and families of problem drinkers.

I'd been a few times before. Dad had brought us to Alateen when we were younger. Although I didn't always have the best track record for attending Al-Anon, I tried to make time, and whenever I went, I was always happy I had. Even if I didn't talk, it was comforting to sit for an hour in a room of people who understood how I felt. It was comforting to know how many people were struggling with addiction, too. I wasn't the only one. But I still didn't know how to work my own 12-step recovery program. I'm still working on that part.

As winter turned to spring and I tried to stop worrying about Mom, I became more attached to Conner. I was thrilled when he sent me emails like, "I'm going to Philly in a few weeks for meetings. Do you and Gizelle want to come? I hope so, because I put Gizelle on the hotel reservation." Then he picked us up in a rental car, the backseat lined in beach towels to contain Gizelle's dog fur, and we drove to Philly where Gizelle ate dog treats shaped like the Liberty Bell. *He is so practical!* I thought. *Liberty Bell, Philly, Conner, Gizelle . . . this is all making sense.*

I couldn't lose him, too. I needed him to provide approval that things were going to be okay. Gizelle and I spent the night at his apartment nearly every night he was in town. I could feel myself morphing from a girl who used to not mind being alone to a girl who was terrified of being alone. Sometimes I picked on him for not being vocal enough when it came to expressing his feelings about me, about our relationship. Sometimes I tried to control him, change him, twist him to fit the image I wanted, which always led to the same arguments: "You pick on me for everything!" he'd say, rolling his eyes at me. "I'm doing the best I can for you. I really care about you. But you always picking on me doesn't help."

Then I'd cry and say I was sorry, that I didn't want to be the type of girl who picked on him for everything. I didn't want to be the needy, nagging girlfriend. That wasn't me. I wanted to be independent and fine on my own. Rebecca always asked what I would do if Conner *did* tell me he loved me more than anything in the world and thought I was amazing. "Could you even say that back?" she asked, looking at me with doubt. "*Do* you love him?" I didn't answer. I didn't know. I only knew I was miserable without him, and that had to mean something, right? I kept going with the relationship. I even invited him on a family trip to the mountains to meet Dad, Erisy, Tripp, and Jenna.

Then one day I was sitting in my closet office in Tribeca when my boss walked in. Derek looked around at the organized boxes stacked on top of each other, the labeled rolling racks, the color-coordinated essential crew-neck tees, and the shoes with matching pairs. "Well. You know how to organize a closet now, don't you?" He smiled, running his hand along the desk that was clear of samples. As I sat there at my computer that day, I realized I did know how to organize a closet. So maybe it was time to leave the closet.

I set off with my resume again and landed an interview with a travel PR firm in midtown. I didn't even know travel public relations was a thing, and I left thinking, *Well, didn't get that job.* A few weeks later they sent an email offering me a position as an account executive. "They've got to be kidding," I told Rebecca, when I read the part that asked what name I wanted on my business cards. (*Business cards!*) I was so excited but also feeling like I must have tricked them or something. It was the perfect job for a girl who loved travel. I worked with a bespoke tour operator called Jacada Travel that offered luxurious, personalized journeys all over the world, and this five-star hotel in Machu Picchu called Sumaq. I studied dream adventures and faraway exotic places. Okay, the job didn't always include a lot of going to those faraway exotic places, but there was always hope that they might send me on an adventure.

Perhaps the best part about my new gig was working in a small office with a boss who adored dogs, so occasionally Gizelle came to work with me. She took the freight elevator up to the fifth floor, where she took her job of sleeping next to my rolling chair very seriously.

I felt like I had control of my life. Boyfriend—*check*! Best friend—*check*! East Village apartment. Career. Dog. *Check! Check! Check!* I was even trying to qualify for the New York City Marathon, heading off for longer eight, nine, and ten mile runs by myself, and shorter, mini high-knees runs with Gizelle.

It was the type of day where it looked like it could rain but the forecast was clear. I unhooked Gizelle's leash, and she picked up speed, galloping in front of me, turning her head to make sure I was following. I sped up until we were

side by side, and then I slowed to my high-knees jog. I
gazed over the water at Brooklyn. A bit of bright-blue sky
peeked through the clouds. I took a deep breath of fresh
air and looked down at my best friend, who was not at my
side anymore.

"Gizelle?"

I looked over my shoulder and saw she was several steps
behind me, walking as though she didn't want her back paw
to meet the ground, lowering it slowly then picking it up
as though the concrete was too hot to touch.

I turned around and walked toward her, kneeling to the
sidewalk under the Williamsburg Bridge.

"Can I see your paw? Your paw okay, girl?" I asked,
thinking perhaps it was something from the streets of New
York City stuck in Gizelle's oversized feet.

I bent my head low to the ground, twisting her back left
paw gently to examine the deep crevices in between the
pads of her foot.

I poked at her limbs. "That hurt, Gizelle?" I asked softly,
searching her eyes, giving her time to respond, always assuming that she would. She panted. "What about that?" I
pressed again. Gizelle cocked her head and looked at me
curiously. Then she nibbled my nose and shifted her body
onto my knee to sit. *This your way of telling me you're
okay?* I rubbed her sides for a few minutes, gave her three
let's-go pats, and she lifted off my lap to begin the walk
home. We got about ten steps, and then . . .

Limp.

The limp was subtle, but it was there.

I called Conner when we got back to my apartment and he rushed over. He watched Gizelle with chin in hand, as I called her back and forth across the skinny hallway. "Oh, I'm sure it's just something stuck in her paws." He kneeled to examine her legs, brushing me off like this was nothing. "Seriously. Odds are, what?—ten to one?—that it's just something lodged in there we can't see," he assured, twisting her paw and narrowing his eyes to study it even closer. He looked like he was doing math in his head as he examined her.

"No, it's not that. I know it's not that." There was a sass in my voice I hadn't intended.

He sat for a moment, seemingly puzzled. "I don't know, then. That's really weird." His lip went tight and he dropped his hands to his sides, stumped. It always worried me when Conner said he didn't know. He was supposed to know everything. Knowing was his best and worst quality.

"I'm sure it's going to be fine. But you could take her to the vet?"

At our first appointment, the vet studied Gizelle's walk, much as Conner had, standing professionally, tapping her chin with her index finger as I marched Gizelle back and forth across the office hallway under white fluorescent lighting. "Okay, thissss way, Gizelle. Okay, now, thissss way. Good doggy." Gizelle followed me anxiously, head high, paws tapping across the floor, which should have been great, except that we were at the vet for a reason.

"She seems okay," the vet declared. "The limping you

saw could have just been stiffness after the long winter. She doesn't seem to be in pain. I would just keep an eye on it."

For a few weeks, I kept an eye on it, and there was nothing to see. Gizelle seemed fine. But then the limp came back again one day in Tompkins Square Park. "Is Gizelle walking weird? Is she dragging her leg?" I asked Conner, flustered, as Gizelle walked in front of us, slightly scraping her back leg against the concrete. I took her to the vet again. The vet studied Gizelle's walk and the response was: Stiffness? Arthritis? Depression? And: "Gizelle seems very in tune with your emotions, by the way she watches you. Have you been depressed, Lauren? She could be latching on to this." And also, "Gizelle has a UTI."

The vets loaded Gizelle up with vitamins and her jillion-dollar UTI meds. I ordered a heated dog bed that apparently helped with joint pain. The vet also advised me to hold a towel underneath Gizelle's back legs on days when the limp seemed worst, like a forklift to help her up and down the stairs of my apartment.

I remained optimistic; the vets didn't see anything too serious, and the limp was just a slight drag of her back leg and always on and off. But whenever I was certain it was gone for good, it came back. So, one day I decided to try a holistic pet shop for recommendations. Conner and I went together. We made our way around the shelves overflowing with organic catnip and biodegradable chew toys to the back of the shop, where a line of owners with their dogs and cats had formed in front of an old man. The man had a mop of white hair and big old-man ears. He sat hunched on a wooden stool in front of a shelf crowded with vitamins, dusty books, and jars filled with colorful powders.

Conner stood thumbing at his phone as we waited, and Gizelle sat at my feet. The woman in front of me rambled anxiously to the man about her Yorkie who kept having panic attacks (coincidence?). The man on the stool listened intently, but showed no sign of sympathy, assuring the lady that giving her nervous pooch Bach's Honeysuckle Flower remedy twice a day would help ease his anxiety. She scurried away thankful, and I was up next. He eyed me suspiciously.

"Hi . . . uh, this is Gizelle," I continued "She's . . . um . . . " But before I could complete that thought, I was interrupted.

"What kinda food ya feeding this dog?"

When I told him, I immediately wished I could take it back. He pinched his face in disgust, then looked at me, "So you're telling me you feed this beautiful dog, this incredible creature you own . . . " He brought his face closer to mine, "*Crap?*" I opened my mouth but only a stutter came out. I could see Conner in a corner a few feet away, shaking his head and chuckling as he stared at his iPhone.

"You're young. I can see that. I can *hear.* What are you, nineteen?" the man continued. "Let me tell you something. This gorgeous creature"—he rested his veiny, wrinkly hand on Gizelle's head—"this dog deserves much more than *crap.*"

I swallowed. I completely agreed. I didn't want to feed Gizelle the crap. But I didn't think feeding her Purina was that bad. She certainly seemed to like it.

Next thing I knew, the man was shuffling in a drawer and pulling out a scroll of empty receipt paper. "Before I can help you, I need you to sign this." He cleared a space to spread out the paper, then read the words aloud as he wrote them one by one.

"I

will

not

serve . . . "

Then he stalled for a moment and tapped his pen to his chin. "What's the dog's name again?"

"Gizelle."

"Oh, right, right, right," he continued. "I will not serve Gizelle any, *ANY*, other dog food except for Blue Buffalo brand."

"Sign," he demanded, tapping his pen twice on the paper. I wasn't about to argue, or ask him about a clause that could include people food. I took the pen and agreed to these terms. The man took the receipt and signed it, too, then he shuffled around the store as Conner, Gizelle, and I followed behind him. I was trying to explain more about Gizelle's on-and-off limp, but while I had this man's attention, I found myself babbling on about Gizelle's occasional smelliness, her UTIs, her constant shedding, her dry nose, how I was looking for something new and organic to clean her ears, and her teeth, etc. He didn't say much, but next thing I knew I was spending triple digits at the holistic pet shop and I couldn't wait to get home with Gizelle to start her new healthy, organic diet. "Thank you so much, sir," I said, practically bowing, taking the bags from the counter.

"That guy is a loon," Conner whispered, taking Gizelle's leash.

The limp didn't go away, so I swung by another vet in the East Village near my apartment. There were two ladies standing behind the desk, one with a thick Jersey accent. She wore lots of sparkly gold necklaces and had paw-print tattoos on her wrist. She kept referring to Gizelle as my *"dawter,"* and I liked that. I asked them to observe the way Gizelle walked. The next thing I knew the lady with the Jersey accent was on the floor behind Gizelle, massaging along her back thigh muscles while I sat in front of Gizelle with my legs crossed on the cold tile floor, petting her and rubbing her ears to make her as comfortable as possible. Then the vet pushed on the part of her back left leg that would be a knee on a person, but on a dog is called the hock. Her lips went tight. She peeked her head around Gizelle and looked at me.

"Heat." She said, pushing the spot again with her thumb. "Yup. There's heat there." She nodded her head with confirmation.

She recommended I take Gizelle to a highly regarded pet neurologist to get it further checked out. What would the neurologist tell me? I asked. Isn't that really serious? Gizelle is only six! How could this be serious?

As fast as I could, I made an appointment with the pet neurologist in midtown. I cabbed us uptown, missing work, only to find out that my mastiff would not fit in their Computerized Tomography machine. Then they reasoned it might be a torn ligament, and if I could let her rest for four weeks and limit walks to twice a day for ten minutes, it might heal on its own.

Might heal on its own? But if not, then what? The vet loaded her up with pain medications, and he said their office in New Jersey had a machine that would fit Gizelle. If I was adamant on testing now, he continued, I could rent a car and drive her there. I swallowed. I felt my lip quiver. "But . . . but . . . test for what?" I asked, as he began going over the different horrible things it could be. I started to sniffle, then a tear. Then I couldn't stop the tears. The vet tried to console me by saying I could choose to wait a bit longer to see if the pain medicine and rest might heal the limp. I sat on the cold tile floor with Gizelle's head in my lap and looked up at the vet. I was afraid, but I couldn't ignore all of the enormous vet bills, so I decided to be optimistic and wait. "It might get better. She probably has not been resting enough," he added. "Don't worry."

But I couldn't not worry. One of my biggest issues was my stairs. Gizelle couldn't rest where I lived. I lived in a walk-up apartment.

"It's my stairs!" I cried. "She can't recover if she's always going up and down on the stairs!" The whole thing was too much. Gizelle kept her head in my lap, almost as if she were trying to console me as I sat there crying in my stupid black work blazer.

"I mean, I can drive her home to Nashville . . . but . . . "

I just kept crying. The vet looked at me like he wanted to help but didn't know how.

I left and called my aunt, because her best friend used to have mastiffs. "How old is Gizelle?" she asked bluntly. "Six! She's only six!" I cried. "I'm sorry but the big dogs just don't live long, honey. My friend lost hers at five." I felt a pain in my chest, and it was then I realized I had always thought Gizelle would live as long as I did.

That night I found myself in bed with my journal. As I wrote, Gizelle propped her chin on the mattress. Her nose sniffed at the edge of the pages. I was feeling so lost and did not know what to do about Gizelle. Kimmy said she could watch her for a couple of days in her first-floor apartment while I figured out a plan, if I needed her to. Conner also offered to help. My dad said I could drive her home to Nashville and he'd take care of her. But I didn't want to put a thousand miles between us. I thought about how my aunt had said: "They don't live long, Fernie." And then I thought about how the vet said it could be something more. I couldn't get those words out of my head.

I looked down at Gizelle, whose nose was pressed to the edge of my journal. My silly journal that contained all my lists. My silly lists of all the things I wanted to do in my life. As I looked into Gizelle's eyes shining up at me, I thought about Gizelle's adventure, the things she would want to do in *her* life. Suddenly my list didn't mean so much to me anymore. Suddenly something told me I needed to make the most of my time with Gizelle.

I started writing down things I wanted to do with Gizelle, and things Gizelle loved to do. *Let's see. What does Gizelle love to do?* Well, she loved to go to Washington Square Park and people-watch, and she loved Times Square in the morning, when it was pretty and rose-colored and quiet. She loved cuddling and dance parties and road trips.

Wait. Road trips. I thought about my nineteenth summer when I'd pile into the car with Erisy, Yoda, and Fatty and drive away. Gizelle loved the car. She hadn't been on a road trip in a while.

10

Road Trip

It was the perfect weekend for an adventure. It was summertime in the city, and Rebecca and I had already made plans to take off work. We were originally supposed to go to the Hamptons for one of her finance guys' birthday parties, to a pretty white house with trendy pool toys in the shapes of swans and doughnuts and pizza. I texted her: "I don't want to go to Sag Harbor with a bunch of snooty girls. We can't even bring Gizelle."

She texted back. "You read my mind."

I called Gizelle's vet. "So, I know she is supposed to stay off stairs, but can she go on a road trip? If I'm really careful?"

"I don't see why not," said the vet.

I texted Rebecca. "Road trip?"

"Road trip."

So Rebecca and I put a Prius rental on a credit card, and we left New York City with Gizelle sprawled across the folded-down backseat.

Our first stop was New York City traffic. Congested bumper to bumper in the rain, I took one look at the cup holder and knew I shouldn't have left it up to Rebecca to get the car snacks. "The kale of the ocean!" she exclaimed, opening up the seaweed chips and placing one on her tongue. I dug through the shopping bag at my feet, hoping to find more than just a second bag of seaweed, but all I found were Milk-Bones. I opened up the box and gave Gizelle a few. She took the Milk-Bone delicately from my hand (like a lady) and with a single crunch it was gone. I was trying to relax, but I felt a tad anxious in the car. *Is this road trip a terrible idea? Am I being so irresponsible? I should probably just be driving Gizelle to Nashville now. I have no plan. I need to get a plan. This is not good.*

The rental's windshield wipers squeaked back and forth and the rain pounded against the top of the car. We did *sort of* have a plan. Well, more of a concept. We knew we were driving north. We knew we were beginning in Stow, Massachusetts, where Rebecca's parents lived, and ending in Kittery, Maine, where Rebecca's sister and brother-in-law lived, but other than that, we were just . . . driving. And we were off to a slow start.

Maybe it was the rain. Or the traffic. Or the grocery stop I suggested we make near New Haven. (I filled a shopping basket with Nutella and strawberries, chips, bologna for Gizelle, turkey for Gizelle, ham for Gizelle, while Rebecca bought the "great chip alternative," carrots.) Or maybe the bologna was to blame. It wasn't doing great things for Gizelle. Every five minutes, a foul scent would seep through the car. *Gizelle! Again, girl? Roll down the windows. Should we stop? Maybe we should stop.*

We'd pull over somewhere in between New Haven and Stow and help Gizelle out of the car like we were lifting a heavy sofa so she didn't put any weight on her paws. Then we'd stand on a patch of grass, and wait . . .

And wait . . .

And wait.

"She must have to go."

"Seriously."

"This is ridiculous."

But she'd only stand and stare at us, panting and smiling, almost as though she was waiting for us to do something. Ten minutes passed.

"Fine, Gizelle. But we're not stopping again. You missed your chance, girl," claimed Rebecca. We'd lift her back in the car. (*Three, two, one, heave! Ow. Ow. Ow. This way. No, this way. God. Shit. Ow.*) We'd drive for twenty more minutes, then our nostrils would flare again. *GIZELLE! Should we stop? Let's stop.*

By the time we arrived in Stow it was 11 p.m. We were exhausted but quick to perk up when Rebecca's mom and dad mentioned there was homemade pizza waiting on the counter. Her dad was on the quiet side, like mine, but that didn't stop him from speaking to Gizelle.

Rebecca's mom, Kathy, was the opposite of quiet. She was a chef, gardener, and outdoor enthusiast, so while we sat eating her gourmet pizza, she rummaged through the closet pulling out everything we needed for our road trip that Rebecca and I had forgotten (or just didn't own): rain jackets, head lamps, flashlights, ponchos, water purifier, compass, maps. She gave us lots and lots of maps, and then spread those maps across the counter telling us about all of the great places in New England we could bring Gizelle. It felt nice to sit in a house at a kitchen counter with a mom and a dad and Rebecca, Gizelle underneath my chair, eating homemade pizza in the warm kitchen light. I threw Gizelle my crust. She missed the catch but was quick to snatch it off the ground. And though I knew I was breaking contract with the guy at the holistic pet shop, I accepted that it wouldn't be the first time, or the last.

After dinner, we followed Rebecca back to her old room. I helped Gizelle onto the bed and we crawled in after her. *Sleepover!* Gizelle rested her head on the pillow next to our heads and lined her body with ours. Rebecca and I climbed on either side and wrapped our arms around her, the three of us tucked safely in a row.

"I'm happy we didn't go to the Hamptons," I whispered.

Rebecca gave my arm a pat good night and I knew she was, too.

The next morning we were off to the White Mountains. It was a three-hour drive and we were navigating with maps. Not Google maps. The ancient paper maps Kathy had given us. That meant making a lot of U-turns—not a big concern because we were certainly having a lot of fun in the car.

"I'm such a sucker for the Dixie Chicks," Rebecca said, turning up the radio and singing along to the twangy music as we wound through deep valleys and forests. When I looked back at Gizelle, she had on a big, dopey grin and her tongue dangled out of her mouth like a tube sock. Maybe this road trip wasn't such a bad idea after all. This was the happiest I'd seen her in a while.

We stopped to do handstands in the grass. We took a nap next to a brook. When we finally arrived in the White Mountains, we took Gizelle to happy hour at the Woodstock Inn and got her a huge bowl of ice water. Rebecca and I ordered two Pig's Ears Brown Ales and clinked them with

Gizelle's water bowl. *Cheers!* It was the perfect day. Just blue skies, a cute mountain man of a bartender in a flannel shirt, and my best friends.

Most of what we did was just drive Gizelle around. She needed to stay off her feet, and the car was an enjoyable way to do that. We drove down the Kancamagus Highway, and Gizelle stuck her head out the window without hesitation, her ears flapping in the wind. Rebecca and I took turns sticking our heads out the window as well, just to see what all the fuss was about. The wind ripped out my ponytail holder and my hair blew wildly around my face. I closed my eyes but could still see the brightness of the sun flickering through the trees. I stretched my arms out the window and felt like I was flying. Fatty was right all along—this felt amazing.

When we passed a sign for Loon Mountain, we realized we didn't know where we were going and pulled the car over. Rebecca was in the driver's seat and Gizelle's head rested on the center console as we uncrumpled the map and held it between us.

"Which way, Gizelle?" I asked, as though she had a preference.

Franconia Notch? But Gizelle couldn't hike. Flume Gorge? Same problem. Santa's Village? Cheesy. Sugar Hill? Rebecca and I looked at each other and smiled.

Then we were off, driving Gizelle to Sugar Hill, for no reason other than we liked the name. We drove an hour, until we reached a hill (hence the name). We wound around a bright-green hill, not knowing where we were going or why we were going there—we only wanted to look out at the world. We drove until the road flattened and we reached a little red barn that was home to HARMAN'S CHEESE & COUNTRY STORE: HOME OF "THE WORLD'S GREATEST" CHEDDAR CHEESE. Rebecca and I looked around and saw nothing but fields of lupine and bright-green grass. Was Sugar Hill only a cheese shop?

Well, Gizelle (. . . and Lauren and Rebecca) liked cheese. So I found my girl a comfortable spot on the patio, and Rebecca and I ventured inside. We sampled "The World's Greatest Cheddar," bought some for Gizelle (another contract breach), and then sat outside on the wooden front porch.

The local Sugar Hill police officer stopped by.

"Greetings, ladies. What a pretty little dog." *Little?* Had we been transported to Gizelle's fantasy land? As he said this, a vintage pink Thunderbird convertible cruised slowly by and tooted its horn. The driver tipped his hat out the window.

"Afternoon, Officer Joe!"

"Afternoon, Sam!"

We chatted with the police officer about the weather, which was clear and blue and sunny—"another perfect day in Sugar Hill." Had we gone into a time machine and ended up in Mayberry?

As we were driving away, Rebecca and I came across a lookout, a wooden balcony built into the side of a hill with a tree stump in the middle. We contemplated whether we should get out of the car again or let Gizelle keep resting. "Just one more view." Rebecca insisted. "We'll be really careful." We sat on the tree stump with "The World's Greatest Cheddar Cheese," a box of graham crackers, and a bottle of champagne Rebecca insisted we pop then and there as Gizelle slurped water from her bowl. *Pop!* Went the champagne. The view from Sugar Hill was so wide I wasn't quite sure where to rest my gaze. The White Mountains stood in the distance beyond a vast stretch of rolling land. The clouds above made shadows on the earth, turning the green treetops to shades of dark blue. "Hey, you should add eat the world's greatest cheese with the world's greatest view to that list for Gizelle." Rebecca suggested, pointing to my journal with her mouth full of cheese and the champagne bottle in the other hand. Then she took a swig.

I sat on the tree stump, rubbing Gizelle's back with my feet, thinking about the things I was escaping, the things I had left behind in Nashville and New York City that I didn't want to face right now, that I didn't *have* to face right now. Not right this second. For a moment, I felt like I had escaped everything. I had escaped the heat in the city. The heat that radiated from the buildings and walls and sidewalks. The heat in Gizelle's leg.

We spent another night in New Hampshire and the next day, as we were driving to Maine, Rebecca looked at her phone. "Oh," she said, turning and smiling at me. "My sister just texted me." She thumbed at her screen. "She said to tell you that you can keep Gizelle at her house for a while if you want. They live in a one story house with a little grassy backyard. She would be happy to babysit."

Rebecca's sister Caitlin had met Gizelle a few times before in New York, and had been looking into getting a mastiff ever since. I really liked Caitlin. The first time I met her I felt like she was my older sister, too, like I had known her for years. She was so calm and motherly. She lived in Kittery, Maine, with her husband, John. I wanted to say no to the offer at first. I wanted to say, *Absolutely not! It's okay! It's fine! We are totally fine and we do not need help and I am keeping Gizelle with me!* But I couldn't. I *did* need help. Gizelle needed a place without stairs, and I couldn't rent another apartment. (I'd already looked into that option.) "Everyone needs help sometimes," Rebecca reminded me.

"But are you sure they wouldn't be inconvenienced?" I asked.

Rebecca shrugged her shoulders. "I doubt it! They have been talking about fostering a dog for so long. You know Caitlin. She and John are the most easygoing people ever. You might as well just check it out and see. They both work five minutes from their house and are home by three every day." I was a weird mix of relieved and overjoyed and sad, but after a moment, not surprised. Somehow Gizelle always seemed to work her magic on people, and somehow Rebecca always found a way to make everything okay. And just when I thought I was running away, it turned out that my escape would end up fixing everything. For now, at least.

We pulled into Kittery, which was a simple Maine town on the water, across a bridge from Portsmouth, New Hampshire. Kittery looked the way I used to draw the world in second grade. The houses had picket fences and roofs that pointed up into perfect triangles. Rebecca and I drove, pointing again and again at how the pretty gray rocks lined the ocean, how the striped lighthouses contrasted against the bright-blue sky, and the way the blue ocean peeked through windows of tall, green trees. With the ocean breeze coming off the water, I could feel my shoulders relaxing, and took what felt like the first deep breath I'd had in weeks. Gizelle was back in goofball mode with a huge, happy grin on her face. When we lifted her out of the car, she walked straight to a pile of grass and rolled happily on her back, not seeming to be in much pain.

Kittery had a couple of bars, a café called Lil's, a locally sourced meat shop (with a dog-obsessed owner), a charming library, and the ocean. Caitlin and John lived on Pleasant Street, and their house looked like a cabin, dark wood with forest-green shutters. It had a fenced-in garden with a hibiscus tree blossoming with pink flowers. As we approached the front door, I could see succulents in the windows and plants hanging from the ceiling trailing long vines. Caitlin and John greeted us at the door. Caitlin ran to give me a hug that lasted just enough longer than normal to make me feel like she understood what I was going through with Gizelle. John was a laid-back, outdoorsy kind of guy. The moment he saw Gizelle, his face lit up. "What's up, GG girl?" he said, laughing at her massive presence, shocked at how big she was as she crept over to him with her tail slowly swinging behind her.

John made fast friends with Gizelle. She wasn't even shy, which was surprising because he was so burly. He bent down to rub her ears and she rested her chin on his knee. As they led us into the house, I looked around and knew one thing had to be true—these people knew how to take care of things. They had bread baking in their oven, and when it was done, served it with homemade jam. The smell of sage wafted through the living room, and I heard nothing but the lovely sound of quietness. No sirens or shouting or loud, crowded sidewalks. It was peaceful.

Gizelle climbed onto their couch and made herself comfortable, and everyone piled around her, stroking her ears and the extra skin around her neck and telling her she was the most beautiful dog in the world. Her tail thwacked against the sofa cushions. Then Caitlin and John went to show us the new vegetables they had from their farm share, asking what Rebecca and I wanted to eat. "Stay there, Gizelle," I told her, needing her to stay resting. Amid our chatter in the kitchen, Gizelle disappeared, and I felt a pang of worry—I was supposed to be making sure she wasn't walking much. We went looking for her and found her in the bedroom. She had helped herself right onto their bed.

They didn't even mind. "Good, girl!" they told her. Then they stroked her ears, cooed at her, and called her GG. I knew letting Gizelle stay here was the right decision. "It's Camp Kittery," Rebecca promised, reaching for my hand as she saw the tears welling in my eyes. "We can come back and visit next weekend, if you want."

So a couple of days later I took a deep breath, gave Caitlin and John the rundown on Gizelle's list of fears, her pharmacy, and her food, asked them to please make sure she stayed off her paws so she'd get better soon. Then I thanked them again, hugged Gizelle quickly, and walked out the door.

11

The Discovery

T hen it happened. That phone call. *The* phone call. Gizelle was in Maine with Caitlin and John. I had missed my qualifying race for the marathon that morning, and when I got back to my apartment, there were the three missed calls. The voicemail waiting. So there I was in my running shoes, standing in the living room back from my run, dialing the number. The phone rang twice.

"Hi, Lauren," Caitlin answered, her voice soft when she said my name.

She explained they were at the vet in Portsmouth, whom they vouched for and whose card had been placed in my wallet some weeks back, where it stared at me every time I fumbled for my MetroCard.

"Gizelle had a hard morning," she continued. "It was like she woke up so much worse, and we just knew we needed to take her in today. We didn't want to wait." I nodded my head and thanked her, and next thing I knew the vet was on the phone.

"Hi, Lauren, this is Dr. Mathewson." His voice also dropped when he said "Lauren."

"Hi," I murmured.

"We—" He cleared his throat. "We really are sorry to have made this discovery with Gizelle." I stopped at the window overlooking the dog run. I felt frozen, as the weekend crowd of canines scampered around below me.

"But Gizelle has osteosarcoma, or primary cancer of the bone origin."

And there it was.

"I'm so sorry you have to get these final results this way.

No one could have identified it sooner for you. Sometimes it just takes longer to identify the disease with these giant breeds." He paused for a moment to wait for me to chime in, but I had nothing.

"We really are sorry to have made this discovery," he repeated.

I hated the word "discovery" in reference to disease. The word "discover" had always seemed it should be followed by wondrous things, like buried treasure, a waterfall in the woods, a swimming hole. But I guess it was a "discovery," like an old bone down in the dirt. The cancer that made Gizelle limp had been buried in her all this time, and this vet had finally dug it up. Dr. Mathewson reminded me this disease was "common in giant breed dogs." He told me the cancer would only keep growing, like it had been all along. The cancer cells would duplicate and invade Gizelle's body. Then cancer would take over, and take Gizelle with it. And that's how it would go with my giant breed dog.

"Unfortunately, this is an aggressive malignancy in dogs with a high metastatic rate." He sighed. "But there are a couple of approaches we can take."

I could amputate Gizelle's back left leg, to cut off the heat. After the loss of the limb, the vet continued calmly, Gizelle would be hit with intense chemotherapy. At this rate the cancer was likely to have reached Gizelle's lungs already, so Gizelle was still unlikely to survive. This was also a lot of pain for her to go through, and not something he recommended for such a big dog.

The other option was palliative therapy, which focused

on controlling the pain and slowing the process of bone loss, with monthly ketamine treatments given to Gizelle through an IV, followed by loads of pain pills, which she'd already been on. With this option she may have another couple months or so left, but that was hard to predict. It could be a matter of weeks. The vet said I would know when it was "time."

I'd known this day was coming, but nothing could have prepared me for it. It was a little like when you are about to jump into the ocean in the winter, and you know the water is cold, but nothing could have ever trained you for the moment your head dips under and the ocean wraps her frigid fingers around your body. Never, ever could I have imagined this news would hurt so badly, that it would take my breath away, that finding out would feel like I could not and would not ever go on. I sat down, and I sobbed.

I don't know how long I sat there, crying. I resented the fact that I wasn't there, that my constant, my Gizelle, was dying and in pain. I was pissed at the vets; how dare they give me hope that this might be a torn ligament! Then I was pissed at myself for thinking that it might be a torn ligament. But that wouldn't change the results. I still wanted to blame myself, wondering if I had done everything for Gizelle that I could have. Dr. Mathewson tried to make me feel better by reminding me that even if I would have tested sooner, it still might not have even shown up yet. He repeated that he was so sorry. Then he described Gizelle as stoic, and I knew that. I was almost bitter about that, too. How much pain had my brave girl endured over the past three months without complaining?

Then, I wasn't mad. I was in a rush. I grabbed my laptop and began to look up the best way for me to get off this island. A bus from Port Authority? Rental car? Maybe a train to Boston and then a rental car? I looked at the clock in the corner of my computer screen and every time it changed, I got more anxious: 12:30, 12:31, 12:32. Tears fell to the keyboard. Every tick of the clock was less time Gizelle had on earth.

Then my phone rang. It was Dad, calling to check in and see how my race had gone. I could barely see the screen through my tears, and my explanation to him was just about as jumbled.

"Slow down, buddy," he soothed.

But I couldn't slow down. There wasn't time left.

"No. I really have to get to Gizelle now. And I missed the stupid race. I'm just going to go rent a car or something." I wiped my nose. "She needs me."

"I'm so sorry about Gizelle. I know you want to leave right away and get back to her. But Fernie, *Gizelle* didn't just find out she has cancer. Know what I mean? This isn't news to Gizelle. Gizelle is the same as she was yesterday in what she knows in life. She's a dog, buddy. She's had cancer this whole time. Maybe Gizelle has known for a while, don't you think? We kind of thought this may happen. You told me you thought something could be really wrong." I tried to take a deep breath on the phone, but I couldn't. I was crying too hard again. Dad suggested I call a few more vets to gather second opinions on the best next steps. I had *time* to get a *plan* in order. I didn't *need* to jump in a rental car right this second. He offered to keep Gizelle in Nashville if that's what I wanted.

I called Conner to let him know the bad news. He was out of town for work. In Disney World. "We got test results and Gizelle has cancer and she is dying!" I sobbed into the phone. He couldn't hear me very well; he was literally walking into the Magic Kingdom, but I remember feeling extra sad that he was in The Most Magical Place on Earth and I was in the worst. "Oh, shit, I'm so sorry, Lauren. Are you going there? Oh, poor Gizelle."

"I'm trying. I'm figuring it out. I don't know what to do."

"Call your boss. She'll understand. She loves Gizelle. Get to Gizelle, you'll feel better." I desperately wished he were with me. How much I wanted him in that moment made me wonder if I really did love him. "Will you tell her I think she's the best dog in the world?" I told him I would.

I hung up the phone and sat down heavily on the dark wooden floor. There were *still* clouds of dog hair under the sofa. I knew that my dad had a point about slowing down and remembering my work obligations. I knew Conner was right about calling my boss and getting to Gizelle.

I called my boss's cell that day and told her the bad news. She told me to do whatever I needed to do. (Thank God she loved our office dog.) I went to work Monday morning to get some of my stuff in order. But I sat at my desk, dazed, tears dripping to the keyboard as my coworkers stared at me. So I collected my things, sent my boss an email that it was too hard to be here, and jumped on the next bus to Portsmouth. I needed to get to Gizelle. I needed to get to Gizelle so I could bring her to the ocean. She had yet to see the waves crashing at the beach.

Besides the driver, I was the only person on the afternoon bus, which was a good thing because I cried most of the way while *The Goonies* droned on the bus TV. *You have the five-hour bus ride to cry,* I instructed myself, immediately deciding that five hours was too long and I needed to cut the tears. I closed my eyes and pressed my head against the glass. When I opened my eyes and looked out the window at the trees rushing by, at the coastal towns along the water, I couldn't help but be reminded of all my times running with Gizelle. Along the East River in the winter, through Central Park in the fall, by the library at night on campus back when I was still a student and life had seemed hard, but I'd had no idea.

Now I was faced with the truth. This was it. The end of our race. She would never run again. I shook my head in disbelief and stared out the window. I needed to find a way to keep putting one foot in front of the other. So, I did the only thing my twenty-five-year-old self could think to do. I dug a pen from the bottom of my purse, shuffled around in my backpack for my journal, flipped to the page that had at some point earned the title "*Gizelle*'s Bucket List," and I wrote.

I stood at the bus station in Portsmouth with my backpack and green duffel, waiting for my bright-red economy-sized Nissan rental car to arrive. "This work for you?" the cute guy in the black suit asked. I eyed the backseat.

"It's smaller, but you probably don't need tons of space," he warned.

I didn't mention the mastiff, but he was right; Gizelle and I had never needed tons of space.

"This works," I said, taking the keys and gunning the car out of the parking lot. It was a ten-minute drive to Kittery. I parked on the road in front of Caitlin and John's house. They'd told me they'd be at work.

"Gizelle!" I called out before even reaching their front door. Pleasant Street was so quiet I could hear her tail thumping from outside. I grabbed the key from underneath the mat where I knew they kept it and swung open the door. She was in the living room on her dog bed, which was a pile of egg-crate mattresses that Caitlin and John had made for her, covered with her favorite red fleece blanket. She lifted herself slowly. I ran to her before she could get up, kneeled down, and wrapped my arms around her neck. "I'm here, Gizelle! I'm here!" Then more quietly, "I'm here, girl. It's okay. We're okay." She put her front paws on top of my chest, pushing me to the floor, licking my face with her long, sandy tongue until I finally sat up and studied her. I thought for sure she would look different—sickly, about to die. But she didn't. She thwacked her tail against the hardwood floor and nibbled my nose and looked . . . the same. Tears welled up in my eyes even though I'd promised myself they wouldn't. I hugged Gizelle again. She rested her head on top of mine and I smooshed my face into her fur. I didn't want to let go. Someday I would have to let go, but not today. Today we still had things to do.

PART II

The Bucket List

12

The Dock

There were many items to cross off Gizelle's Bucket List, but the first item I wanted to complete that day was the beach. I'd always wanted to go to the ocean with Gizelle. I figured she might enjoy standing in front of a big body of water that would make her feel small. Plus, there are no scary buses at the ocean. Only sun, sand, turquoise water, and waves. *Waves.*

We found a dog-friendly beach at a place called Fort Foster Park, and I organized a beach bag for Gizelle with all the care of a neurotic helicopter mom. Water bowl, extra gallon of water, beach towel. *Check!* Glucosamine, gabapentin, Rimadyl, tramadol. *Check!* I brought her chicken from the Maine Meat shop, her dog bone and red rope toy. Then I packed my gear: camera, journal, sandwich.

I parked as close as I could to the sand, then lugged everything across the parking lot at turtle speed. I didn't want to move too fast and make Gizelle feel obligated to keep up. Her limp was only slight that day, but the vet had told me it was important to be extra careful of both her back legs. The left hind leg would only grow weaker, and if she injured the right while trying to stay off the left, that would be it.

We walked a dozen or so yards until I came to a quiet stretch of sand in between some rocks where I threw everything down. Fort Foster Park was beautiful. There was an old, run-down lighthouse off in the distance in front of us, black boulders dispersed across the sand, not many people, and a beautiful blue line where the ocean met the sky.

"Look. What is it, Gizelle? It's the ocean! See the ocean?" I pointed.

I walked down to the water as Gizelle sat at our little camp a few yards away and watched me. "C'mere, Gizelle! C'mon, girl!" I coaxed, wiggling my fingers in the water. The water was calm and not too cold. Gizelle looked at me for a moment, pausing to sniff the air before approaching the surf. "C'mon, girl! You can do it!" She lowered her head slowly to examine the water, tail still tucked, prob- ably wondering what this enormous tub was doing here and why it seemed to be moving. She crept closer, but when the first teensy-tiny wave spilled gently to the shore, just barely tickling Gizelle's front paws, her eyes widened, she turned around and retreated. I shook my head. *Same old Gizelle.* Once that wave was gone, she tried again. Then pulled back. Approached. Pulled back. Approached. On Gizelle's fourth try, her eyes were on me. "Come on, Gizelle!" I clapped my hands. "C'mon!" She walked farther and farther, right into the ocean. I held out my hands, clapping. "Good girl! Good, Gizelle! You did it!" I cheered as she stood there, panting and smiling, before trying to drink the ocean.

We stood for a few minutes, admiring how the sun glis- tened on the water. I wondered if Gizelle felt small. I felt small, but also free from troubles. For a moment, standing in front of the ocean, I didn't need to fix anything. And despite the horrible circumstances that had brought us here, I was still at the beach with my best friend on a weekday, digging my toes into the wet ocean sand.

Gizelle shook dry as we walked back to our little camp. I ate my sandwich and gave Gizelle her medicine wrapped in a slice of deli meat and treats from the Maine Meat shop. I wrote Gizelle's name with some seashells in the sand. We took a nap. After an hour or so passed, we carefully walked back to the car and I lifted Gizelle into the backseat, wrapping my arms around her waist, casually, as though we did this all the time, so she wouldn't be embarrassed. *Three, two, one, heave!* I thought as I hoisted her into the car. I climbed into the front. I was plastered with dog fur; there was salt on my skin and sand in my hair. I picked up my journal and looked at the list. "Go to the beach." I crossed it out, feeling happy and accomplished that I had just done something simple with my best friend that I'd always wanted to do, and it seemed like she'd enjoyed it.

Our adventure continued. We spent the next week discovering Maine. Gizelle and I found the best lobster rolls (Clam Shack in Kennebunk), the best doughnuts in the world (Congdon's Doughnuts in Wells), twisted through roads with views of the sea, explored antique stores trying not to knock things over (Gizelle) and not to get taken in by "collector's items" (me). We met goats and chickens, got lost on purpose, and sat in a garden watching butterflies. I kept busy by coming up with bucket list things for Gizelle to do, trying to get creative with things that didn't require walking, which did help take my mind off the pain of losing her.

As we drove back to Kittery, I found myself glancing at Gizelle through the rearview mirror of the rental car.

She sprawled across the backseat with her nose peacefully propped against the window ledge as she watched the greenery pass by. I couldn't stop worrying about how much longer she had. A week? A month? What if she was feeling pain and unable to tell me, and how would I know when to finally let her go? She was on pain medicine and receiving monthly doses of ketamine, but, still, was she okay? My mind felt filled with uncertainties, but it all came down to one certainty that was the hardest. I was going to lose Gizelle.

Clouds turned gray up ahead, and as a storm blew in I realized I couldn't make my pesky worries stop. My worries had even expanded into things that hadn't even happened yet, things that might never even happen. *What if Gizelle breaks her good leg? What if Mom drives drunk and hurts someone? What if my boss actually hates me because I'm missing work, even though she said it was fine? What if Gizelle dies tomorrow? I'm making Gizelle a bucket list so she can "live in the present"? But doesn't Gizelle already live in the present? This is stupid. I am stupid.*

I kept driving, and as the rain finally subsided, a sign on an old house caught my eye: FRISBEE'S 1828 MARKET, AMERICA'S OLDEST FAMILY STORE. I turned the car around. One item on Gizelle's Bucket List was "Eat ice cream." Maybe now was a good time to stop? I went in and grabbed a pint, stood underneath the Frisbee's sign, trying to decide where Gizelle should enjoy the Ben & Jerry's vanilla ice cream, when I noticed a wooden boat dock behind the store. A bit of sun hit the wood and turned it a warm, inviting gold color. I got back in the car and drove us down the tiny slope of a hill in the parking lot so Gizelle didn't have to walk. Then I helped her slowly out of the car. The ocean breeze kissed my face. It was salty and warm.

Fishing boats tapped against the dock and seagulls flew out over the water toward the horizon as I stepped onto the wooden planks. Gizelle's toenails clicked behind me, her back left leg slightly dragging, which put a kink in her usual trotting rhythm, but her tail still swung behind her. Even though it was nothing more than a little boat dock behind America's oldest family store, this spot seemed so magical that I almost felt the need to whisper.

I sat on the wood and Gizelle plopped next to me in a sphinx position, chin up, watching me with anticipation as I peeled the plastic off the carton and removed the lid. I took a bite with the white plastic spoon, then looked at Gizelle, who was watching the spoonful of ice cream with the same look of desperation and determination she always had, as though if she looked at it long enough, it would miraculously become hers. I waved the pint in front of her, and she followed it back and forth with her head, licking her chops. "You want it, girl? You waaaaannnt it?"

Her tail whipped the wood once with excitement.

As I held the ice cream in my hand and looked at Gizelle, I thought about my worries, how heavy they were. Then I thought about how light and easy this moment felt. What purpose did my worries serve me here, now? The only thing my worries could possibly do was prevent me from enjoying this dock with Gizelle. So, I politely asked my worries to please stay on land for a moment while I cherished this precious moment on the dock with my dog. And for once, my worries listened. It wasn't like my mind clicked into some euphoric life-changing yogi calmness, but for twenty minutes or so, I wasn't lost in my mind's rabbit hole. I was in the present.

I placed the pint in between Gizelle's paws. She dove in with her long, slow tongue, angling her muzzle toward the ice cream as the carton rolled across the wood. I laughed, and then I cried a few happy tears as the lobster boats went by and she slurped the ice cream.

I let her have at it with Ben & Jerry for a moment, took a few photos, then held the pint steady to her snout. Now I knew that Gizelle and I had a new secret spot on the seacoast of Maine behind America's oldest family store. I slid my spoon inside the carton of ice cream and smeared some ice cream on her nose. She slurped it off. "Good Gizelle." I laughed.

13

A Dog's List

Maybe a bucket list for a dog was a silly thing to do. Maybe Gizelle didn't have dying wishes. Maybe Gizelle wasn't even supposed to eat Ben & Jerry's. Some angry man once told me that making a bucket list for a dog was selfish. "That list is all about you!" he exclaimed. "A dog bucket list is only for the human!"

Maybe he had a point. I instantly thought of the Trader Joe's dog biscuits I always bought Gizelle. The treats were shaped like cars and shoes, fire hydrants and squirrels ("things dogs love"), and every day I looked at Gizelle and asked, "Now, which one do you want today? The sofa? Or the squirrel?" Then one day it seemed silly. Gizelle didn't have a clue what these shapes were. This dog biscuit shaped like a squirrel was shaped like a squirrel for me. Not Gizelle. Maybe it's always about the human (and the dog is the more-than-willing participant). I *knew* Gizelle couldn't write a bucket list. Gizelle was a dog. Dogs cannot write.

But sometimes I liked to imagine Gizelle *could* write. I liked to believe that if I said, "Hey, Gizelle! Write your own bucket list, okay, girl? Write down everything you want to do in your life," Gizelle might have some difficulty coming up with her own list. She had never been much of an alpha. She followed me everywhere and always seemed to want to be doing whatever I was doing. Gizelle would probably be the girl peeking over at my page to copy everything on *my* list.

So *if* Gizelle was copying my list, my list said:

Bring Gizelle on a boat

I always wanted Gizelle to ride in a boat. Maybe it was because we loved watching the canoes in Central Park, or because my mom had always told me mermaids were real (and I had this obsession with *The Little Mermaid*—when much, much younger, of course). At first I was dreaming big. A dog-friendly cruise through the tropics? Could we finagle our way onto one of those shiny white yachts in Battery Park City? But the more I thought about it, this *was* Gizelle's Bucket List. A cruise was way too much work for a sick dog, and those loud ship horns were more terrifying than any bus honk in New York City. Plus, Gizelle couldn't walk much on land. I wasn't about to test her sea legs.

Then one weekend Conner and I wound up in Moulton-borough, New Hampshire, with Gizelle. We rented a rickety old house with roosters in the front yard and a pond in the back. We were standing barefoot in the grass, the summer sun beating down, planning to lie out near the water when I spotted it. There, in the shade of overhanging trees next to the pond, was one large plastic canoe.

In an instant I envisioned the three of us floating through the pond together on the canoe as Conner paddled. Gizelle loved the car; how could she not enjoy the light breeze from a canoe ride? I hated that she couldn't run anymore. Gliding in a canoe would be a way for her to keep exploring new sights and smells without having to walk.

"Conner. We have to get Gizelle in that canoe."

Conner looked at me, then eyed Gizelle, who was standing at my side, with her back left leg floating in the air, careful not to put weight on it.

"She was afraid of the grill yesterday. You really think she'll want to canoe?"

"If we get in the canoe, she'll want to get in the canoe."

We walked slowly down the yard to find that the vessel was wedged in the mud, covered in spider webs, inhabited by a number of six- and eight-legged creatures, and filled with stagnant, swampy brown water.

"Are you sure *we* want to get in that canoe?" Conner mumbled. I nodded, explaining it was for that whole Gizelle bucket list thing I was doing, half-joking, but not joking at all.

"Oh right, right, right. The *bucket* list," he said, turning to address Gizelle. "Well, if it's for your bucket list, Gizelle . . . " He smiled.

Conner set his backpack on the dock and tottered into the water. He was shirtless and his hair was messy, so different from his city uniform. He even had a beard growing on his face. I liked this look—tan and rugged, standing in the mud on the lakeshore. I watched as he wriggled the boat out of the sticky mud to dump out the mucky water. Gizelle studied him, ducking slightly when he lifted the canoe. Then he took a dirty old orange lifejacket and swatted away some of the spider webs and insects. Conner pulled the canoe deeper into the water, then held it steady with both hands.

"You jump on first, Lauren. Call Gizelle. And I'll lift her over," he directed.

I stepped one foot in, grabbed the lifejacket (pillow for Gizelle), then encouraged her to follow, clapping my hands over the canoe and saying, "Come on, girl!"

She sniffed the edge and then gave me a puzzled look.

"C'mooooooooon," I soothed. She hesitated at first, but then lifted her front paw.

"Good girl! Keep coming." I held the canoe steady as Conner rushed to wrap his arms around Gizelle's fragile second half to hoist her in carefully. She was quick to settle into her place, a curled-up ball on top of my feet. Conner climbed in next, grabbing the paddle and his backpack. At first we stayed close to the dock, just in case she hated it. Conner and I sat facing each other and Gizelle lay between us, looking at me.

As we slowly paddled across the pond, Gizelle lifted her head and surveyed the horizon, ears forward, eyes focused. I watched her carefully, hoping she was enjoying this, and when her mouth opened to a pant where I could see her teeth and her jowls curved upward in a smile, I knew she was. Conner and I paddled her around the edge of the pond. We looked for beavers and other wildlife, listened to the birds, and watched a few mallards float alongside us. We drifted through a field of pretty water lilies spread across the surface of the pond.

"*See, this is just like that scene from* The Notebook," I

imagined Gizelle saying as she propped her head on the side of the canoe, a light wind tickling her jowls.

"She likes it!" I couldn't help telling Conner as we cruised back into the middle of the water and pulled the paddles in so we could float wherever the slight current took us.

I closed my eyes and stretched out my legs, leaning my head back to enjoy the warm sunshine of the late afternoon on my face. Conner cracked open two beers from his backpack. It was quiet, a quiet that couldn't be found anywhere in New York City, not even in Central Park at night.

Gizelle rested her head on my thigh and gazed at me. I rested my hand across the back of her ears, stroking softly. Every muscle in me felt calm, like my insides were made of butter. We floated for what seemed like a long time when—

THWAK! Conner smacked the canoe with the paddle.

WHAM! He smacked it again, cursing under his breath.

"*What* are you doing?" I gasped, as Gizelle pushed into me, scraping her claws against the plastic and trying to stand, which caused the canoe to rock.

"Spider!" Conner shouted back, lifting his feet to hit the canoe repeatedly like a game of whack-a-mole. "Damn! Missed it! Shit! Missed it again!"

Gizelle continued scrabbling against the canoe. We rocked heavily from side to side, making waves in the once tranquil pond. Water sloshed in over the canoe's edge. Beer was spilled.

"Stop it! Stop it!" I yelled at him, placing my hands over Gizelle so we didn't have a mastiff overboard. "Swim" was not something I wanted on Gizelle's Bucket List, and "Rescue limping mastiff from pond" was not something I wanted on mine.

"You're freaking out Gizelle!" I screamed. "You're freaking out Gizelle— Oh! Oh! Oh! SPIDER! Spider, spider, spider. That's a huge-ass spider! Oh my god. It's on Gizelle. It's *on* Gizelle! Oh my god!"

The spider had a fat body the size of a walnut, and he was hairy. He skittered across Gizelle's back. Then he jumped. I grabbed the lifejacket. "Shit! Shit! Shit!" I swatted Gizelle softly yet mindlessly—attempting to brush the spider off.

"I'm sorry, girl! Sorry! Sorry!" I yelled, taking one final swing that ended the poor guy's life, right there on the wall of our canoe. Conner loosened his grip and wiped beer from his lap. I exhaled. Gizelle looked around. Then resettling herself and relaxing pretty quickly, she rested her chin on my knee and was back again to her smiley pant as though everything was fine. I set down the lifejacket. The spider's once-scurrying legs were now smashed across the side of the canoe. I felt bad. "Maybe that's enough canoeing for Gizelle's Bucket List," Conner offered. I nodded. I couldn't stop looking at the spider. Hopefully canoeing with a mastiff was on his bucket list.

A couple of weeks or so later, Rebecca left New York to come up to Camp Kittery for more of Gizelle's Bucket List adventures. Her mom and dad even drove up from Stow.

I strolled to the Maine Meat shop in Kittery and picked

up a gleaming hunk of beef—a well-marbled slab of grass-fed rib eye with a lovely swath of fat attached. The woman behind the meat counter, who knew Gizelle's order by now, told me I "couldn't go wrong with this eighteen ounces of pure heaven." I hoped she was right about that whole "couldn't go wrong" thing because unless adding Itso Hot Sauce to takeout ramen or cooking quinoa in a teakettle counted as culinary skills, my kitchen expertise left quite a bit to be desired. The audience gathered in the kitchen as I unwrapped the raw meat from the white paper and told Gizelle this was all for her, not entirely worried anyone else would be fighting over my first rib eye.

I cranked up the stove. It made a bunch of intimidating clicking sounds before it suddenly lit. I threw a bit of butter in the cast iron, then tossed in the meat. *Ssss!* The steak sizzled. I waited, then flipped the meat every fifteen or so seconds like one does with a pancake. My first rib eye, for some reason, was looking more like a fast-food hamburger patty than the pretty steaks with argyle char pattern that my dad used to prepare back in Tennessee. The smell of seared meat and fat permeated the kitchen air as Gizelle sat intently, leaning into my leg with her nose touching the kitchen counter, her ears pushed forward, eyes on lock, as if the meat were about to scurry across the pan.

"Almost ready, girl." I told her, giving her head a pat, as I turned off the stove and poked the meat with my finger. It seemed to be the right amount of springy. Its outside was brown, with pink peeking through the cracks. "Medium rare okay, girl?" I asked. She didn't glance away. Yes, medium rare would do nicely.

I slid the spatula under the meat and tossed it onto a plate. Rebecca rested her chin on my shoulder and peered at my masterpiece. She stared at it for a second and when I looked at her, we both chuckled.

"Gizelle, she worked wicked hard on that steak, okay?" she said, patting Gizelle's head.

"Yeah, Gizelle, this isn't a steakhouse steak, it's not Conner's Michelin-starred leftovers, and it's not Dad's, but I worked hard on this. I made it especially for you," I told her, walking out to the backyard as Gizelle and the rest of our new family followed.

I stood barefoot in the grass with the plate out in front of me like a tray, realizing we hadn't decided whether we should cut the meat up and feed it to Gizelle in bites or give it to her whole. We went back and forth, but then we imagined Gizelle in the backyard thrashing the full piece of meat in her mouth, ripping it apart piece by piece, savoring its juiciness as if it were a wild animal dangling from her massive jaws. *Let's give it to her whole.* The audience stood and held iPhones and cameras in front of their faces. I dangled the eighteen-ounce rib eye over Gizelle's head as she opened her mouth, her brown eyes so wide the whites peeked out.

"Okay, girl!" I beamed. "Here it comes . . . " I released the meat from my fingers, and like a pebble dropping into a well, the steak disappeared. Gizelle swallowed it like a Tylenol, without one chew. We stood in silence for a moment, and then Gizelle's audience slowly lowered their cameras. Rebecca tilted her head curiously, squinting at Gizelle. I imagined the steak floating in her tummy like an inner tube down a winding river. Gizelle looked up at us with concerned, eager eyes, as if to say, *"Can I have another bite?"*

\

14

The Leaves Turn

"What are these orange blob things, Lauren?
Should we be concerned?"

Contrary to the vet's prognosis—that Gizelle might not make it to the fall, it was October and she was still enjoying life. I found it hard to believe that last Halloween I was researching costume ideas thinking, *We'll show those lobster Chihuahuas who's boss.* And now it was Halloween season again, and I was researching more ideas for a Bucket List, trying to show cancer who was boss, grateful Gizelle was still here at all.

"Make Gizelle the firehouse dog for the day!" one friend suggested. Sirens? Burly men in big hats? Fast, unpredictable trucks? Let's not put Gizelle's worst nightmare on her bucket list.

"What about Doga? It's yoga you do with your dog." *Oh!* But what kind of poses?

"Take her to the little-dog park—let her be her true self for the day." We'd tried that once. Those Chihuahuas were pissed.

"Skydive?" Ummm . . . as much as I would like to give Gizelle the ultimate head-out-the-window experience . . . No.

"Grill a steak?" *Check!*

"Netflix night?" *Check!*

"Share pasta like Lady and the Tramp! . . . Have a dance party! . . . Find G a boy!" *Check, check, check!*

Then I received a text from Dad.

"See fall foliage with Grandpa? LOL Dad"

Dad had still not figured out the meaning of "LOL," but his feelings about Gizelle had come a long way since she was "that big puppy" and just another enormous reminder of Mom's lax parenting. Even though I wasn't entirely sure his motives were *all* Gizelle, given that he hadn't visited me in a while, and Gizelle was colorblind and therefore didn't see reds and yellows as we did, I couldn't agree more. Watching the leaves change sounded like the perfect addition to Gizelle's Bucket List. So Dad booked a flight from Nashville to New York and soon we were driving up the coast of Maine away from Camp Kittery with Gizelle in the backseat.

Mom and Dad were officially divorced by now, which was more of a relief than anything else for me. I'd never seen my parents happy or laughing or lounging on the couch together in front of a movie as I saw my friends' parents doing. I knew my mother and father didn't get along. "Can't you just divorce her?" I'd bluntly ask my dad in college, whenever Mom was acting up again. He'd always tell me it was more complicated than that. Then he'd remind me there'd been a time when they'd been happy, and maybe I didn't remember. But divorce finally happened, after five years of them being separated and twenty-eight years of marriage. And their divorce didn't faze me much.

I knew a little about Dad dating other women. He had just visited Erisy in Santa Barbara and she reported that he kept taking selfies and sending them to a woman named Linda. Tripp, Jenna, Erisy, and I chuckled about it over texts with one another: "Dad? Dating? A woman named Linda?" As though he was only supposed to be our dad and nothing else. We were happy for him, but it was still weird to think about him with other women. He moved on from

Mom, and sometimes I was jealous he could divorce her and cut ties and find someone new. Sometimes I wished I could move on from my mom, too. But I was still hurt and mad and confused by her, and I desperately wanted her back.

We hadn't booked accommodations for the night, which was rare for Dad, who liked predictability, especially in the "knowing where I'm going to sleep tonight" department. Tourist season in Maine was winding down, and as we rounded the curve of US Route 1 in Cape Neddick, I noticed a driveway leading to a collection of tiny white cottages. Spread among a clearing surrounded by bright-yellow trees, the cottages sported rocking chairs out front and sky blue shutters. It looked like a place out of a magical storybook, it was mastiff friendly, near the ocean, and within five minutes we were the only people staying there. Gizelle and I unpacked our bags, claimed a spot on the foldout couch, and strolled outside to look at the trees.

When I noticed a pile of golden leaves in the distance, I had to resist my childish urge to run and jump in, knowing that my large shadow would do her best to run after me. So I walked slowly, with Gizelle at my heels. Her back left leg barely brushed the ground anymore, unable to support her weight. What the vet had described as mere heat was now a visible, egg-sized bulge protruding from Gizelle's hock. I missed the sound of Gizelle's paws thundering against the dirt. I missed us chasing each other in the park. I missed running together. But we waded into the pile of golden foliage slowly, and once we were standing side by side, there was no need to avoid the childish urges anymore.

"Ready, Gizelle?" I spread my arms and sat down heavily into the crunchy pile of leaves. Gizelle plopped right on top of me.

"Okay, okay, girl. This is fine. You can sit here." I rubbed her sides. Then I looked up at the sky and watched a yellow leaf float from a branch, twisting and dancing through the air. A red one followed. Then a burgundy.

As I watched the colors falling from the trees, I thought about how something could turn so beautiful right before it went brown and left the world forever. Kimmy once told me that leaves were the only thing that were most beautiful before they died, but when I heard a heavy rustling in the leaves next to me, I knew this wasn't true. I looked over at Gizelle, who had climbed from "her seat" and was now rolling on her back in the leaves, belly to the sky, legs spread in total unladylike fashion. Her tongue dangled from the side of her mouth, and her jowls revealed her bright white teeth. There was foliage clinging to her jowls like a beard. She was panting and smiling and as beautiful as I'd ever seen.

The next day, the clouds moved down from the sky and stretched across the Maine coastline. It was chilly and raining, then sunny, then sleeting, then foggy, then raining again. All in one day. All we did was switch the windshield wipers from on to off. Dad was new to the idea of a dog bucket list but excited when I assured him that Gizelle's Bucket List was quite flexible—you can make things up as you go, and Gizelle enjoyed doing the same things over.

We found the best lobster rolls, again and again, and then another time. We visited our favorite empty, rocky beach while my dad took pictures, holding his iPhone far out in front of his face and staring at the screen, smiling, while I attempted to lure Gizelle near the waves again.

"C'mon, buddy, let's all take a beach selfie. Get in here, Gizelle," Dad said as he met us at the shore, kneeled in the sand, and stretched his arm in front of us, angling to fit Gizelle's head in the frame and struggling to make his finger hit the right button. I laughed and rolled my eyes, somewhere in my mind marking that taking selfies with Dad on the beach was a nice addition to Gizelle's Bucket List, and maybe my own, too.

"It's pretty sweet, the way Gizelle watches you, Fernie," he told me back in the car.

I smiled at him and reached back to pet Gizelle on the head.

"She watches you so carefully. Like she's your mom. I don't think I've ever seen an animal watch someone the way Gizelle watches you." Then he said how happy he was I had her in Knoxville and New York with me because he knew "the big puppy" always kept me safe. He told me he was sorry she wouldn't be around forever. My stomach lurched when he mentioned the Gizelle-going-somewhere part, but I let out my breath and kept my hand in the backseat stroking Gizelle's head, trying to focus on the present moment.

We spent most of our time driving through the coastal towns, admiring lighthouses, listening to Jimmy Buffett.

We watched surfers, fed seagulls fries, fed Gizelle fries, fed ourselves fries. I took my dad to Gizelle's dock behind America's oldest general store. Then we stopped at a tiny pub near Kennebunkport. It was raining. The ceiling was low and the floors were a red, creaky wood. Gizelle sat underneath my barstool. I sipped on a pumpkin ale, and Dad had the lightest beer he could find. Gizelle had more fries. Lauren did, too.

We wound around Wells Beach and Dad made a fast U-turn when we passed a pumpkin patch in front of a white church with a tall pointed steeple. We parked the car and walked Gizelle through the pumpkin patch in the drizzling rain to let her pick out a pumpkin, which ultimately meant we watched her roll in the grass until she toppled over a pumpkin and was slightly startled by it. "That's the one!" I cheered. The pumpkin was square shaped, muddy, rotted on one side, and missing a stem. "It's perfect, Gizelle," I assured her, wiping some of the mud off it and onto the grass, then tossing it in the rental.

After long days of short walks on the beach, meandering drives, and hot meals, it turned out our nights, sitting at a tiny table in the tiny kitchen, were what I loved the most. Gizelle lay underneath the table, with her head resting across my feet. Dad took a sip of his leftover, twist top Miller Lite he'd saved from the night before, and I opened another pumpkin ale. "Rummy?" he asked, splitting a deck in two and shuffling it on the table.

He dealt.

I lost.

I dealt.

I lost.

I kept losing.

I rubbed my feet on Gizelle's extra neck skin, and she nibbled my toes. "I keep losing, Gizelle!" The light from the little lamps and the yellow walls created a comforting glow. I peeked out the window at the wintry darkness that was creeping over our temporary little corner of the world. The outline of bare branches silhouetted against the black sky and the remaining leaves shivered in the wind. Deep down, I knew that if Gizelle saw the winter, she wouldn't see spring.

We sat at the card table for a few hours, and soon the conversation turned to Mom. There weren't many people I spoke to about Mom. I was embarrassed: My mom was a drug addict.

"I'm mad at her," I told Dad. I looked around the little beachy white cottage and thought how much my mother would love being here if she were sober. "She's missing everything. She's missing her whole life. It's so sad." I stared at my cards, bitter about all of the years I'd spent picking up my mother's messes, when I was the one who still needed a mother myself.

I thought about the day I'd gotten Gizelle. Even though my mother was struggling with addiction at that point, we were still best friends. She was still there for me. And now Gizelle was reaching the end of her life, and for the past six years, my mom's addiction had gotten progressively worse until one day I'd woken up and realized we weren't close anymore. Mom had missed family reunions and weddings, a friend's funeral, Mother's Days, Thanksgivings, Christmases, her birthdays, our birthdays. She wasn't there and often if she was, she wasn't sober. Sometimes she'd just offer to send money or a gift to us in an attempt to still be supportive, and while that was generous of her, it wasn't a substitute for having her around. I'd much prefer having her around. I wondered if she would be at my wedding, or see me have kids. I didn't understand why she couldn't just get her act together.

Dad was less openly emotional when it came to Mom. He always listened if we needed to talk about her, and I'd never once heard him say anything bad about her, despite her always talking bad about him. I knew he thought we shouldn't play the pity card, that we shouldn't be victims, and that we should be strong and grateful for the things we had. But that night Dad responded.

"Does it help you to see Mom like she has a disease?" he said, staring down at his cards. "You know—maybe a little like the one Gizelle has?"

It certainly wasn't the first time I'd heard addiction referred to as a disease. But it was always hard to see my mom as truly sick. Over the years I'd watched her struggle in countless ways—through rehab, DUIs, broken promises, jail, halfway houses, therapy, doctors, AA meetings—but the addiction had always won. I'd heard all the promises— "I'm better! I'm fine! I'm going to meetings! I'm going to visit you! I'm going to teach aerobics again! I'm going to volunteer at the animal shelter! I'm going to move to California! I'm going to *visit* you! I'm going to visit you and Gizelle!" But she never did any of these things. I never believed her anymore. It was too hard to have a relationship with someone who seemed to lie about absolutely everything.

But what if, deep down, she wanted all of those things to be true but just couldn't figure out a way to make them true? What if she really was sick, lost in her own mind and unable to get out? What if drug addiction wasn't embarrassing at all? What if I could try to see the struggles my mom was facing and rather than add to them, try to see her with empathy and compassion—the way we view people who are plagued with sicknesses? On one level addiction is so self-indulgent, so it's tough to see it as a disease, but I also know it takes more than willpower for people who struggle with it to get better.

It made sense that Mom was sick. Like cancer, addiction had side effects, side effects that morphed her body into someone unrecognizable and prevented her from acting normally. Like cancer, it was confusing to understand and heartbreaking to watch. Like cancer, some got better. Some didn't. Like cancer, maybe it was okay to just be sad about it. Maybe it was okay to accept that there was nothing I could do to change it.

Many people argue addiction isn't a disease, that it's a choice. Even some alcoholics say they don't want to be called someone with a disease. But I think that if addiction were a choice, my mom would be better by now. I don't think my mom *wants* to keep picking the drugs and the alcohol over me. I think she is lost within the depths of her own struggle and can't get out.

Dad told me that he thought addiction was a little bit like being lost in a maze, and if I tried to fix Mom, I would only end up lost in the maze with her. And as much as I wanted to cure my mother, to fix the problem, there was a sense of relief to be found in letting go, accepting that I didn't have to.

I couldn't change that Gizelle was sick, and I couldn't change that Mom was sick, any more than I could change that the leaves were turning and falling from the trees. And maybe doing absolutely nothing about my mom's addiction was actually doing everything, because it was letting myself out of her maze so I could move on and be grateful for the wonderful things that did exist in the world—lighthouses, pumpkin patches in the fall, seagulls at the beach, a mastiff snoozing across my feet, card games with Dad in Maine.

That was the whole point of my dog's bucket list, right? I couldn't change Gizelle's cancer. I would never cure Gizelle's cancer. I could only change my attitude toward Gizelle's cancer; it could either bring me down or become my excuse to live life fully with Gizelle while I could.

I listened to the tree limbs scrape against the walls of our cottage, and after a dozen losses and one small win, I threw in the cards.

"'Night, Dad." I said, patting his shoulders.

"'Night, Fernie," He stood and hugged me good night,

kissed my forehead, and screwed the top back on his second Miller Lite and placed it back in the fridge for tomorrow.

The vet had told me it would be obvious when it was time to let Gizelle go, that her quality of life would disappear. When Gizelle didn't want to get up for normal things like dinner and bedtime and treats, we would know. I walked into the bathroom, and as I was standing in front of the mirror with my toothbrush, I heard a slow clicking of paws approaching. Gizelle stood for a moment, then pushed her big black snout up against the crack of the door. *Sniff. Sniff. Sniff.* Then she let out a short, sad moan. I laughed and opened the door. She walked in, pressing me into the sink, yet still managing to find space in between me and the shower. Then, when I walked to the living room to our fold-out couch, she backed out of the bathroom and followed me there, too, resting her chin on the bed. "Ready, girl?" I asked, wrapping my arms around her back legs and hoisting her up. She crawled to the top of the bed on her stomach and rested her head on the pillow. I was little spoon this time. She placed her paws around me and rested her head on my cheek. I turned to face her, curling up in the extra skin around her neck. And that spot, under a mastiff's big head, with her jowls draping over my face like a blanket, had to be one of the safest places in the world.

15

A Snowfall

Wells Beach, Maine

Gizelle's breath broke through the cold, making little white clouds in front of us. It was December, my mastiff's last Christmas, and Conner and I were bringing her to Wells Beach in York County, Maine. The cancer on Gizelle's back leg had grown to nearly the size of a pool ball, causing her leg to float uselessly in the air behind her. She was having difficulties standing up to go to the bathroom, and she didn't like leaving her bed. The life was fading out of her, and I knew it.

"Watch a snowfall on the beach," I scribbled in Gizelle's Bucket List, still trying to avoid the thought of losing her. Rebecca had once told me that watching it snow on the beach is the most magical thing in the world, because it's two of nature's most wonderful things happening simultaneously. I thought Gizelle and I should experience this, and I wanted Conner to be there, too. He was a shield from the pain of losing Gizelle and losing my mom and being stuck with myself. He was a cover-up over the loneliness I was afraid to feel. In a way, holding on to him was my last chance at keeping control of the world around me.

Conner opened the back door of our Ford Focus with a sweeping hand, a chauffeur's gesture.

Gizelle, a pro at this by now, stood by the backseat waiting for me as I curled my arms under her waist, heaved her gently into the car, and climbed in after her. Gizelle and I organized ourselves across the backseat, her massive head snuggled against my chest, my arm around her like a boyfriend's, stroking her ear, as Conner drove up I-95.

"How's Gizelle?" he asked.

"She's okay," I responded, smiling weakly into the rear-view mirror and snuggling my head closer to hers. She turned her snout to lick my cheek. Her licks were long and slow, and she licked with her whole head, moving it up and down with her tongue, almost with purpose.

In the backseat of the car, I thought about the kind of love I had for Gizelle. There was nothing she could ever do that would change the way I felt about her. It didn't matter that it was a pain to wake up in the morning when I was late for work and walk her in the rain, waiting for her to sniff the few trees and many trash bags that lined Forty-Third Street. It didn't matter that I swept up clouds of brindle fur in my apartment and scraped dried dog drool off my walls every night, or once went to work with slobber in my hair. It didn't matter that her number twos were so large someone once told me they needed their own zip code, that my apartment turned into a Slip'n Slide every time she drank water, or that she wasn't the neatest eater, so sometimes I'd step on half-chewed food and it felt like mashed potatoes in between my toes.

I hated to imagine life without Gizelle. I did not want to let her go. But in the back of the car, driving up to Wells Beach, when I thought about life without Conner, I realized I didn't feel the same way. I wondered if and when I'd ever be brave enough *to* let go.

I'd originally planned this weekend to go out to see Gizelle in Maine by myself, but was now really the time to be alone? Conner was my safety belt. He was helping me through the hardest thing I'd ever faced. I had no plan B without him. I was terrified to lose him. So, I created all sorts of optimistic expectations for a romantic weekend together, instead. And driving up the coast of Maine to Wells Beach, looking down at my green duffel bag on the floor of the rental, I could practically see my expectations for the weekend packed right into it.

I had my beanie, the one I planned to wear on the cold beach, snuggled arm in arm with Conner, sipping a carefully selected Cabernet. He'd wipe a snowflake from my cold cheeks, kiss me, and tell me he loved me. I had lingerie that I had bought with him in mind, dainty, red, with Christmas-y lace that I'd purchased from a tiny boutique on Second Avenue and had felt like such a grown-up doing so. I had packed my journal that contained Gizelle's Bucket List, which left no room for crying and instead listed all sorts of festive holiday ideas such as:

Meet Santa

Cook a lobster dinner

Pick out a Christmas present from
     Scalawags Pet Boutique

Visit a Christmas tree farm

Cuddle

Watch the snow fall on the beach

Perhaps I envisioned the weekend with Conner like some sort of Nicholas Sparks book. The synopsis would read something like: "Reeling from the heartache of her dog's bone cancer, she thought Conner might be wrong for her, but after a cold December weekend on the beach in Maine, she realized he might be just the one who could save her."

When we arrived at the Lafayette Oceanfront Resort at Wells Beach, an old white motel sitting right on the sand, a few isolated lights glowed in the parking lot, but everything else felt abandoned. Only a sliver of the moon appeared behind a black cloud, and it was hard to tell where the black ocean ended and the sky began.

"We can add 'Stay in a beach motel' to Gizelle's Bucket List," Conner threw out, pulling Gizelle's weekend bag out of the trunk and helping the sweet girl out of the car. The winter wind blew in from across the sea, tossing my hair chaotically into my face. I squeezed my arms to my chest to keep warm and took slow steps with Gizelle as she limped across the parking lot into the motel.

The room had pastel walls, a blue love seat, and a bed-spread printed with fading water lilies. Outside, the wind raged at subzero temperatures. Inside, we all launched into motion: Gizelle headed for the love seat, I made a beeline for the closet and put on a pungently bleached white robe, and Conner popped the bottle of Billecart-Salmon champagne that he had brought.

"To Gizelle," we toasted, holding our cups to her as she casually backed herself into the chair without taking her eyes off us.

Conner went into a one-sided discussion of the chalky, citrus notes in the champagne, the nose of ripe pear with touches of hay or something, while I went into a one-sided discussion with Gizelle's floppy ear, asking her if she wanted one of the grass-fed hot dogs I'd brought her from the Maine Meat shop. I held the meat in front of her nose. *Ah yes, nose of pork grease with no hints of powdered preservatives, a lingering note of smokiness on the finish. Hmmm... also a touch of hay?* Then I sent the hotdog into the large cave of her mouth.

Next, Conner opened a bottle of Cabernet. He poured it into the two plastic motel-furnished cups, took a sip, swished it around in his mouth like mouthwash, and nodded his head, pleased. "Should we take Gizelle out?" he asked. I put on my clothes and he handed me the glass of wine, nudging me to guess if it was Old World or New World.

We slid open the glass door that led us right onto the sand. The white tips of the waves rolled on the black water. We couldn't walk far with Gizelle, so we stood and looked at the dark ocean while she sniffed the salty air. Everything was like I'd imagined it would be. There was the spicy (Old World) red wine, a patch of moonlight peering through the clouds, the sand and the sea, Gizelle, Conner, cold winter night. It should have been perfect! But there was no kiss. No butterflies. No telling each other we loved each other. We talked about wine, Conner's HR director, my boss, and I picked up Gizelle's poo from the sand. Then we walked back to the room. Conner was snoring in minutes. The lingerie I'd bought stayed wrapped in its pink tissue. Gizelle curled up in her big blue throne by the bed next to me. I closed my eyes but didn't sleep. Something in me finally clicked, and I wished I were alone. I wished it were only me and Gizelle here this time.

When morning arrived, we drove to the seaside town of Kennebunkport to check out the annual Christmas prelude. All of downtown was overflowing with holiday cheer. There were red bows wrapped around lampposts, jingling horse carriages, and wreaths hanging from quaint wooden buildings. There were carolers and drumming soldiers and dogs wearing elf shoes.

Conner did everything right. He waited in line at the Dock Square Coffee House and brought out surprises—whipped cream in a cup for Gizelle, hot chocolate for me. He held my hand. He constantly held the iPhone out in front of his face to snap photos of me and Gizelle together, directing us to stand in front of the Christmas tree decorated with colorful buoys, pose by the beach chairs, and then next to an enormous wreath. "Gizelle, look here! Look here, Gizelle!" He yelled in a high voice, waving his mitten in the air. We made sure Gizelle got plenty of downtime to sit in the grass and people watch. We tasted the spicy chili from the annual chili competition, bought Gizelle another hot dog, and answered the usual English mastiff questions passersby couldn't contain themselves from asking.

Yes, she eats me out of house and home.

No, no, pony rides today.

Why yes, she does weigh more than me. Thank you for asking!

But then there was a new question, one I hadn't heard much of until now. "Why is your dog limping?" I wasn't sure when it became polite to point out others' disabilities, but I didn't want to tell them the truth. I didn't want to face the truth.

"She has a torn ligament. It will heal. She's fine!" I fibbed (despite knowing I shouldn't).

Then I patted Gizelle's head as she leaned into my side, warming me with her big brindle body as the people walked away.

I kept at it with Gizelle's Bucket List. Next up was a Christmas present from Scalawags Pet Boutique, a fancy dog store in Kennebunkport with gourmet treats and fashionable dog clothes. "Gizelle, what do you want for Christmas, girl?" I asked as she sniffed at some of the lobster plush toys and lobster dog hats. I showed her a bright-red lobster rope toy that seemed like a slam dunk, but she didn't show much interest. She turned her head away and went sniffing to the back of the store until she found a wall filled with Christmas sweaters. She sniffed at the clothes, sat, and then looked at me with sad, desperate, please-can-I-have-one eyes.

Great. I thought. *Gizelle wants a sweater and I bet they don't have a plus-sized section.* It turned out that I'd underestimated the pressures of capitalism, and soon Gizelle was trying on all sorts of sweaters: a pink one that said Kennebunkport that didn't fit around her neck, a gray argyle sweater that I would have worn myself, and then, the crown jewel, a red fleece sweater. I slid her paws in carefully, one by one. As I stepped back to snap pictures of her in the sweater, thrilled that it fit and matched her red rope toy and favorite blanket, a saleswoman came over and beamed at Gizelle:

"Oh my gosh, the Golden Paw fleece sweaters?" She clapped her hands in front of her face with delight. "You are just going to love that sweater, big puppy. It looks beautiful on you!"

Then the saleswoman leaned in toward me, and with her voice low like she was telling me some sort of secret, she said, "That really is a great sweater. She'll be able to wear it for years."

She'll be able to wear it for years. I looked down at Gizelle in the pretty sweater, and right there in the back of the Scalawags Pet Boutique, next to the wall of rainbow-colored dog clothes, my heart cracked. No, she would not be able to wear it for years. Would she even be able to wear it next week? *How much longer, Gizelle? Tell me. Promise you'll tell me, okay?* I thought, knowing that if she could, she absolutely would. I paid for the sweater, a little unable to figure out exactly why I was spending forty dollars on this, and slowly we walked out the door.

The weekend carried on. We drove to the supermarket, where I rolled up my sleeves and picked out three lobsters from the tank, always feeling like if I ate lobster, I should be able to brave cooking it myself. And also that if lobster is the grandest meal a girl can have, Gizelle should have it, too. (Certainly fresh Maine lobster wouldn't be considered a contract breach, right?) We met up with Conner's local friends and cooked a feast. I put Gizelle in a lobster-claw headband and a white lobster bib and drank more fancy wine. When we sat at the table, I listened to Conner and his friends carry on about business and money, and I wished we were talking about something else *during* the feast, but it was okay. Gizelle sat at my feet, and I threw her pieces of the soft white meat, that she polished off quickly.

After dinner, Gizelle and I cuddled in her big blue chair, and I gazed out the window at the empty beach as the matte-gray sky turned to a wintry moonless black. Then I looked at Conner in bed and thought about all of the nice things he did for me and Gizelle. How he bought us treats and drove us out of the city, manned the lobster dinner and many other dinners, surprised me with coffee in the morning, helped me budget my first salary, walked and baby-sat Gizelle, ruined my taste buds so I no longer wanted Two Buck Chuck. But there was still this tiny voice inside that told me something was missing from this relationship, that all of the things I liked about Conner were based on conditions. And no matter how many dinners he bought me or how many things he did right, the little voice inside that kept telling me to leave was never, ever going to go away.

It was Sunday, our last morning at the motel. I woke to the sound of ESPN blaring from Conner's iPhone. I lay on my stomach on my side of the bed, Gizelle on the blue chair next to me. I tapped her head softly with my fingers. She opened her eyes, brought her snout to the edge of the mattress, and rested it there so we were nose to nose. Her warm breath touched my face.

I flipped my head to face Conner. Conner's back was pressed upright against the headboard, glasses on, studying the phone screen in his hand. "I think I'm gonna go walk Gizelle on the beach.," I told him, my voice groggy from sleep. He took a second to respond. "It's so cold, though," he said, eyes still on the phone. "Why do you want to walk on the beach when it's so cold?" He turned his head to look at me.

"C'mon, Gizelle can wait." He put his nose toward my face to kiss me on the lips. I touched his stomach gently. "No, no, she can't. We already missed sunrise with her. It's our last morning here."

"Gizelle is *juuuuust* fine in her chair," Conner confirmed confidently, setting down the phone, sliding his hand down my chest to untie the glaringly white bathrobe.

I turned my eye toward Gizelle; she was watching us. What I really needed was for her to take me for a walk. I needed air. I put my hands around Conner's cheeks and pulled his head close to my face. "I'm just going to leave for a minute," I promised, not being able to tell him that I actually wanted to *leave* leave. Hardly even able to admit to myself that I wanted to leave. All I wanted to do was exit the room for ten minutes to be with Gizelle.

I slipped out from underneath Conner and rolled off the bed. Gizelle's head lifted from the chair when she felt me move, and her eyes followed me around the room as I collected my clothing, in a race to catch the morning. I tripped over Gizelle's bowls in the bathroom and splashed water on my feet. I threw on leggings and the first shirt

I could find, forewent a bra, and grabbed the winter coat that I had carelessly flung on the floor. I grabbed my gray knit beanie, barely tied my boots and let Gizelle go au naturel, leaving her collar and leash behind. I didn't even put on her new red sweater! "C'mon, Gizelle. C'mon, girl," I grabbed a handful of neck skin and eased her off her throne. I slid open the heavy glass motel door and we slipped through the thick, long blue curtains and out onto the beach.

The cold air hit me like a wall. The wind blew straight through my hat and coat, raising goose bumps. The tide was down, so the beach was long. All I wanted was to sprint to the water, twirling and jumping and dancing along the shore, Gizelle kicking at the waves with me, bounding up in the air with the ocean at our feet. All I wanted was to run with Gizelle. But Gizelle could barely walk. Her tumor was the size of a fist, and it felt like we were both stuck in leg irons, restrained to small movements and short distances. We would never run together again. I looked out at the long shoreline of the empty beach, then down at the wet sand beneath my feet. There was nothing left to do but sit.

So I sat in the cold sand, slapped my hands to my face, and cried.

I'd been running with this dog bucket list idea in an effort to be strong, to choose happiness and cherish life with Gizelle, but reality was catching up with me. Gizelle's cancer was something I couldn't run from anymore, like the cold, like my relationship. I made a fist and tucked my hands into my coat to try to stay warm. My cheeks were cold, my feet were cold, my teeth were even cold. What the hell was I doing out here on this freezing empty beach alone? How had I even ended up here in Maine? I looked over at Gizelle. I was about to get up and head back inside to the motel room when Gizelle limped over to me from a rock inspection a few steps away.

She licked my teary cheeks, and then she turned around and backed up into my lap and sat on top of me. She had been my protector, my confidante, my greatest burden and my biggest pride, and now she was my heater, too. Sitting on the cold beach in Maine with my massive English mastiff on my lap, I wasn't quite sure how I had made it from Tennessee, to New York City, and now to Wells Beach in December, with Gizelle. I still didn't know what I wanted to be or do, who I was or where I was going, but I felt like whatever it was wasn't in that motel room anymore. I had brought Conner because I didn't want feel lonely, but I had somehow ended up on a cold empty beach, wondering if I was feeling more lonely than I would have if I had come alone.

I wrapped my arms around Gizelle and locked my fingers at her chest. Her heart beat against my palms. She was huge and soft, warm and comforting. I cried into the back of her brindle coat. "I love you, Gizelle." Maybe that was the only thing I really knew that day.

As I sat with her, crying, I looked up. It had started to snow. The snow fell on Gizelle's fur and melted next to the wet patch my tears had made on her back. The delicate crystals of ice stood out on her long, dark lashes. They sat on her black muzzle, next to little gray dog hairs. Rebecca was right. Seeing it snow on the beach in the winter was one of the most beautiful things in the world. I smiled and shook my head, wiping my eyes with my sleeve. It was then I realized that I always wanted to be the one to take Gizelle on the adventure, but maybe she took me on one.

Gizelle had kept me in the cold long enough to witness the snow, and I almost felt as though she were telling me something. *See, Lauren, I brought you down here to get you out of that room and feel what real loneliness is on this big empty beach. I'm going to sit in your lap right now and be here for you, but soon you will see that you can handle this. Soon I won't be around, but you're going to be fine by yourself. You'll be okay. The pain won't last forever. Nothing lasts for very long.*

I guess when you bring a dog into your life, you are setting yourself up for heartbreak, aren't you? Sure, you will most likely have to say good-bye and it will be the saddest day ever, but it's so worth it, isn't it? To have a dog. To learn from their unconditional love. That morning I wondered if most romantic relationships were the same. Maybe Conner had helped me grow up and had provided companionship when I'd needed him, but maybe it didn't have to last forever. That didn't mean it had been a waste. Maybe none of our relationships are wastes; maybe everything puts us one step further in the right direction.

And when I thought about the love for my brindle puppy on the beach that day, I realized that if it was love I was after, if my own bucket list really did say, "Fall in love," perhaps I needed to finally let go of Conner in order to find it.

16

Let Go

A few weeks passed. It was the first week of January. We dimmed the lights in the kitchen, lit candles throughout the room, and pulled out the fancy china. I made one last trip to the Maine Meat shop. Then I stopped at the wine shop, where I sifted through wine labels, splurging on a bottle of 2008 Barbera, and silently caught myself thinking about how Conner, my ex, would be proud.

Conner and I broke up after our trip to Wells Beach, but it took us months to actually cut ties completely. We tried to "just be friends," but we always ended up sleeping together. Then we finally realized if we actually wanted to move on, we had to stop hanging out. He asked one day if I would ever consider getting back together with him, if I would ever change my mind, and I desperately wanted to say yes because I knew if I said no that would be it, he'd disappear forever. But when my mind went back to that morning on the beach with Gizelle, when I was freezing and lonely and scared and uncertain but somehow seeing things crystal clear on that sad, frigid beach in the winter, I knew what my answer was. I knew in my heart we weren't right for each other and we'd never be right for each other. There was no point in putting it off anymore, no matter how hard it was. I had to be brave. So I said no, and he moved on.

I set Gizelle a plate at the small wooden dinner table, next to mine, in between Caitlin and John. John grilled the steaks. "Have a fancy dinner," I scribbled in her bucket list. It was the only thing I could think to do on Gizelle's last night.

We had learned our lesson the first time this item appeared on the bucket list, and I wasn't about to give Gizelle another eighteen-ounce single bite of steak. So I set her a plate at the table. Gizelle lay on the floor near my feet. She didn't want to sit up and prop her nose on the table to smell the food like she used to. She didn't follow me into the living room. She didn't want to stand over her bowl to drink water. She remained with her stomach pressed to the floor. It was time. We sat at the dinner table and toasted to Gizelle. I cut her filet into bites the size of Frosted Mini-Wheats. One by one, I fed her pieces of steak with a fork. I brought each bite down to her mouth, and she opened her jaws slowly around the end of the utensil, slid the bite off with her white teeth, chewed and swallowed. Good girl.

I fed her slowly, not wanting the meal to end, but soon I looked down at my plate and there was nothing left. Stomach full and as content as I was going to be on Gizelle's last night, I picked up the plate and set it on the floor next to her so she could be dish washer. Caitlin and John did the same. We leaned back in our chairs and sat in silence, listening to her clean our plates with her tongue.

Then it was our turn with the dishes. One by one we lifted ourselves from our food comas, picked up the plates from the floor, and stood in an assembly line of scrubbing and drying as Gizelle sprawled back on her side across the kitchen, barricading us by the sink. None of us minded. I let her have a tiny bit more ice cream from the pint, and then it was bedtime. *Please not bedtime,* I thought, knowing this night wouldn't just end another normal day. It was the closing curtain.

Caitlin and John stacked foamy egg-crate mattresses on the floor of the office, and we padded them with every blanket and pillow we could find. I crawled on the makeshift bed. "Come on, Gizelle, come on!" She hobbled into the room, and her paws went:

tap

tap

tap

tap

on the wood floor one at a time until she reached the bed and plopped down. There was no pretense at a trot in her step anymore. Every step she took looked like she had to work to deliberately take it. It looked painful for her. I didn't want her to be in pain.

I pressed my cheek to the pillow and rubbed my hand in a circle on the sheets next to my face. "Come here, girl." Gizelle crawled to me, snuggling in close, her nose touching mine so I could feel her breath warming me like a heater. I buried my head in her chest. I loved the smell of Gizelle. Even her breath was oddly comforting. I remembered the smell of her puppy breath—a warm, milky honey—and all the other smells we had discovered together: Marc Jacobs Daisy perfume floating around sorority girls at UT, the greasy breeze billowing out of the 99 Cent Express Pizza, the urine of Tompkins Square Dog

Run, the crisp air at the top of Sugar Hill. Of all the smells we now knew by heart, her breath was the one I wished that I could bottle and save.

"Good night, girls," Caitlin ventured, peeking her head in through the door. I turned away from Gizelle and looked at Caitlin with wet eyes. She paused in the doorway and tilted her head, gazing at me consolingly. "If Gizelle lived in the wild, she probably would have already passed. Probably walked away and fallen asleep in a field somewhere? Right?" I nodded my head slowly, unable to bear the thought. "It's time," Caitlin promised. Like Rebecca, she had a way of speaking with a calm, slow assurance that always made everything feel okay. "This is the right thing. Don't worry, Lauren." Then she came over to caress Gizelle. "You're the best dog in the world, GG." She turned off the light and closed the door.

I switched on the little lamp next to us, grabbed my journal from my black backpack, flopped onto my stomach, and, as always, used Gizelle's side as a desk.

January 6, 2015

Gizelle doesn't know she will die tomorrow, but I guess most of us don't, do we? I don't want to lose her.

Gizelle taught me to try to be as good as she thinks I am. She taught me to think beyond myself. She brought me to Maine, helped me see the ocean and the coast and smile and laugh and explore. She helped me remember I am an explorer, but I want to keep exploring with her. I don't want to say good-bye.

I lifted myself to sit cross-legged and watched Gizelle breathe—loud inhales and exhales that reminded me of those deep cleansing breaths of yoga practitioners. Every time I blinked, more tears ran from my eyes. I rubbed her back, just with the tips of my fingers, like my mom used to rub mine, tenderness in every stroke.

I kissed the tips of my four fingers and touched my hand to the place her limp started. "I know it's there. I know," I promised her. "It's going to feel better soon," I whispered, sniffling. All along I had been hoping she trusted that I did know her cancer was there and that I was doing my best to take care of it, that maybe I wasn't always perfect but I tried my hardest and loved her more than anything. I dropped my head next to her nose, took her paw and wrapped it around me, and snuggled myself into her big warm chest until she lifted her head and put it on top of mine, as I knew she would, as she always did and would have continued to do until the end of eternity. We fell asleep.

My alarm buzzed at 6 a.m. I didn't lift my head from the pillow to turn it off, just thumbed at the phone to make the thing hush. I'd had a plan for Gizelle's last morning, because it had to be special. Sunrise on the beach—January in Maine. We would go on a little car-ride adventure. Coffee/bagel run, a little like Mom and I used to do, and then we'd sit on the beach one last time and watch the black sky fade into a wintry, lavender gray. We'd watch the moon disappear into the morning. Our last night closing like a show in front of our eyes.

But the thought of unwrapping myself from Gizelle's paws, of unwrapping Gizelle from her peaceful slumber, did not sound fun at all. Plus, it sounded like the Arctic tundra outside. Cold Maine winds howled through the trees and bristle branches scraped against the roof. What were we going to do? Shiver on a dark beach . . . again? Would it actually be *that* magical? Hadn't we already done that?

Gizelle was snoring her cacophonous, preposterous snores, her jowls spread flat across my pillow. "Gizelle, Hi Gizeeeeeelllllle. Wanna go see the sunrise?" I whispered, touching my pointer finger to her whiskers. She cracked one eye open, left the other squished into the pillow, and let out one more longer, louder snore followed by a look that seemed to say *Are you kidding me, Lauren? We went to the beach* yesterday. *You also took me to our dock behind Frisbee's* yesterday. *And it's* freezing *out there.* So I thought about a simpler, ongoing item on Gizelle's Bucket List: "Cuddle." I turned off our alarm, wrapped myself in her paws, nuzzled my head back underneath her head so I was as close to her warm breath as possible, and we fell back to sleep, without feeling an ounce of guilt. We snoozed until 10:30, until the smell of coffee woke me up.

I shuffled into the kitchen, my morning hair a mess on my head, to find Caitlin and John sipping green smoothies from pretty blue cups. They handed me one consolingly. I took a little sip but wasn't hungry. Then I was back at it with the meat for Gizelle. I had picked up one final sausage from the meat shop. I fired up the cast-iron skillet and soon had the sausage sizzling. I put it on a plate trimmed with blue hydrangeas. Then I stood with the empty cast iron in my hand, wondering what else I could cook in it. What else could I do for Gizelle before she left us?

Caitlin and John had both adjusted their work schedules so we could go to the vet together. We had planned to bring Gizelle first thing in the morning, but then we second-guessed ourselves.

"Should we wait until the afternoon, try and enjoy the morning with GG?" John suggested. "I don't want to rush it." We looked at Gizelle lying on the floor and paused for a moment, as though giving her time to chime in. I decided not to answer for her this morning. Instead, I sat still and ran through Gizelle's Bucket List in my head, thinking of all the things Gizelle and I had managed to get through in her short, beautiful life.

Survived college
Moved to Times Square
Moved to the East Village
Ate New York pizza
Grilled a steak
Had a lobster feast
Went on a canoe
Ate ice cream on a dock
Had sleepovers

Cuddled

Danced on rooftops

Explored Central Park

Reached Number sixty-seven on Buzzfeed

Picked out a pumpkin

Ran

Went on road trips

Watched the waves at the beach

Sat in the snow

I carried the list in my head, happy that I had everything written down and could try to think about life in such a simplified way. Maybe life didn't have to be so complicated after all. Maybe life could just be a list of simple, special adventures? But I still didn't quite feel ready to give Gizelle's list up. "Gizelle, what do you think?" I asked in a high voice, a little bit shaky, as her jowls remained glued to the floor and she lifted only her eyes to look at me.

"Wanna go outside, Gizelle? Let's go outside." We helped her up from the ground, and John followed us out, carrying her back end down the single step to her mini yard that had turned into an ice-skating rink. Gizelle struggled to squat on the ice.

"Feel better, lady? Good, Gizelle! Good girl!" I told her when she managed to stand, trying not to act sad in front of her. She gave a slight wag and a pant.

"GOOD girl!" John added.

"Good Gizelle!" We chimed in together, cheering her

on as we would a toddler. Our voices got higher and our breaths broke through the cold. A tear trickled down my face, but we just kept telling Gizelle how great she was and how much we loved her. We didn't know what else to do in that moment. We were both so sad, but also just wanted to be in the backyard with her one last time. We didn't mean to get Gizelle excited. We weren't thinking about how stoic she was. Gizelle wagged her tail from side to side on the ice. I clapped my hands and told her she was such a good dog. Gizelle gave one last big, excited jump and then:

YELP! YELP! YELP! YELP!

Her noncancerous leg buckled, and she collapsed onto the ice. We ran to her in horror, and her whole body rumbled into a violent shudder as we helped her up. She shook it off. Then she dropped her head, embarrassed, probably ashamed that she could no longer be what she wanted to be—playmate, protector, running partner, confidante, friend. John and I also lowered our heads in shame—we should have known better. When John started crying, I was so sad, but I also knew how lucky I was that he came into our lives. I knew how much he loved Gizelle, how he came home from work every day to see her. I was so thankful to have him as dog-godparent, to have him as Gizelle's other dad. I knew they had a special bond, too. "It's okay, girl. It's okay," I whispered, rubbing her ears as quiet tears trickled down my face. That was it. It was time to go to the vet. I'd given her all of the protein, car rides, beach trips, and snuggles that I could. If it were my bucket list, I would keep writing, more, more, more adventures with Gizelle! I *need* Gizelle! But if this were Gizelle's Bucket List (which I suppose it was), she would probably say, "Okay, that was a great adventure! Thank you! I love you! Now let me go, Lauren! Let it all go, Lauren."

Let her go.

It was the only thing left to do.

Except for all those other only things left to do. We turned the heat on in the car to let it warm up. We packed her dog bowl away so we wouldn't have to come back and look at it. I cleaned up the mountain of blankets to keep sad leftover dog hair to a minimum. I packed away her pills and her treats and I wiped nose marks off the cabinets. Each of us took turns crying. It became clear how Gizelle hadn't just influenced my life; she had influenced theirs, too. It was a testament to what kind people they were, some of the kindest I'd ever met. Not many would volunteer to babysit someone's gigantic, terminally ill dog. Gizelle's life came with an unpredictable ticking timer and a pharmacy that had to be restocked with pills every two weeks, and those pills had to be wrapped perfectly in peanut butter to get the patient to swallow them. Caitlin and John did this. They were the best godparents a young dog mom could have asked for, and I said a prayer of gratitude for them as I tried to reach the car without breaking down.

I lifted Gizelle's bum into the backseat of the car, placing my feet shoulder-width apart, tightening my abdominal muscles and bending my knees and hips into a squatting position to lift her. *Three, two, one, heave!* It was the last time. Whenever I did this, I always feared that I would drop her before we reached the seat, but I never did. Lifting her into the backseat always made me feel strong, motherly. I climbed in the back with her. She settled in and snuggled her head in my lap. My bottom lip quivered. As Caitlin started the car down Pleasant Street (which seemed to be much too cheerfully named) and we headed toward the vet's office, I understood the meaning of the expression "a broken heart." My heart hurt miserably; it felt as though someone had tied a belt around it and was pulling tightly. It was the worst feeling I'd ever felt. I collapsed my chest onto Gizelle's head. I pinched my eyes shut.

17

Run

By the time we got to the vet, the sun was piercingly bright, beating into my eyes like bright stadium lights. "Okay, Gizelle. Go potty!" I sniffled, shuffling my feet in the grass on the lawn outside, breathing into my hands to try to keep warm. I'd never wanted to stay outside in the cold so badly.

Going inside meant that it would be over, that it already was over. Going in meant that there would be no more Lauren and Gizelle. There would only be Lauren. I loved being Lauren and Gizelle. I didn't want to just be *Lauren*. A huge part of me didn't know who that even was. Gizelle walked toward the doors. They were drawing us in like a sneaky riptide. Suddenly, I was standing inside—I didn't even remember walking in.

"I'm here with Gizelle . . . I have to . . . We have to . . . It's . . . It's time . . ." I choked on the words. My cries sounded like hiccups now, like short little whimpers. A man in blue scrubs handed me a box of tissues and didn't ask questions, just shook his head in sympathy. "I'm so sorry, dear. Hi, Gizelle. Follow me," he said softly, leading us into a dimly lit room with a big black CD player and a soft gray couch. Gizelle limped slowly behind.

It was the saddest make-believe living room ever. I wondered how many hearts had broken in that room. There was a curtain over the door to give us privacy, and thick blankets on the floor for Gizelle. But Gizelle, oddly determined, limped to the corner of the room to lie down. She watched the door. I wondered if she was already on her way out then. I wondered if she was trying to get a head start. I brought a bone for her to enjoy. She looked at it but didn't chew it. It sat like an accessory, a prop, next to her. She almost seemed too distinguished to stoop to chewing a dog bone, beyond canine, beyond human, in fact. She just lay there, with her head up and her eyes on the door. I called her over to the blankets.

The three of us crowded around her. My face was smeared with tears and snot. I looked over at the CD player, feeling guilty for not bringing her theme song, Whitney Houston's version of "I'm Every Woman," or Stevie Wonder's "For Once in My Life." I wondered what other kinds of songs or noises had played on that CD player in this pretend living room. The silence felt right, in any case. I sat and held Gizelle's paw, rubbing it softly with my thumb. "It's okay, girl. It's okay, girl" I repeated, unsure who I was speaking to—myself or my dog.

Then the vets started to put on what I can only describe as a very well-rehearsed and thoughtful performance. They began to enter and exit the room with a carefully choreographed series of questions and explanations, always sincere yet so calm. I could tell they had done this hundreds of times, which was comforting. It seemed as though they began and ended every sentence with "I'm so sorry," which I never got tired of hearing. I was sorry, too.

They asked if we wanted to give Gizelle a sedative so she could fall asleep—not the death thing yet, just sleep—and then we wouldn't have to worry about her stressing and hiding in the corner when they came in with "the syringe." "I'm so sorry." There were decisions that I was not prepared to make: what to do with Gizelle's body, what kind of urn I wanted, did I want an expensive private cremation or was I okay with a group one? "I'm so sorry." But I couldn't answer their questions. All I could think about was soaking up these last few minutes with Gizelle. So they let me check a box saying that they would call me in a few days to talk about it. "I'm so sorry."

I sat on the floor next to Gizelle, rubbed her ears, and marveled above all her beauty. Even in the horribly sad end of her life, when she was crippled with pain, she was still my brave, jowled, magnificent, big-boned, curvy gentle giant—my Tyrannosaurus rex, Jumanji, Smartcar, Beowulf, Bear, Gorilla, Tiger, Holy Shit, AHHHHH!!!, King Kong, Cujo, GIRL YOU CRAZY. My pretty brindle, daughter of Dozer, once scared of the sound of wrapping paper but then brave enough to move to New York City. My therapist, my BFF, my confidante, and the noble keeper of every secret my nineteen to twenty-five-year-old self ever could have had, so thank goodness she was so big. I know I will love again, but never will I love anything the way I loved my 160-pound puppy.

The vet gave her the sedative and wrapped her paw in a hot-pink bandage. I couldn't help but be pleased at the color. "This isn't it yet," she promised. "Gizelle will fall into a nice little nap right now. She'll just drift to sleep, and then I'll do the rest. I'm so sorry, guys."

I nodded my head *okay*. One of my hands rested on the floor next to Gizelle's paw, and the other I kept on her head, stroking her softly. I watched her get very sleepy. Her breaths started to slow and her whole body began to look heavier, impossible as that is to imagine, as though she were sinking into the floor. Her eyelids began to flutter. Just as I thought she would fall asleep and never move again, she picked up that big head of hers and placed it on the palm of my hand, and there it stayed, some part of her always having to touch some part of me. I unraveled. My whimpering turned to tears and I wept. I was holding her whole, big heavy head in my single hand, the weight of it pressing against my fingertips. "It's okay, Lauren. It's okay," I bet she'd say. I could feel her breath in my palm, moistening my hand. Her breathing got slower until I could only feel a light wave of hot air in my fingertips, disappearing but then reappearing again like the ocean to the shore.

The vet pulled out the syringe. "She won't feel any pain. But before I do anything, I want to warn you, there's no telling what may happen when she passes. Her bowels may move, she may urinate, she may shake a little bit. She won't feel any pain, though. I'll insert the needle, and in about twelve seconds it will stop her heart. I'm so sorry. It will be okay. Okay?" I nodded yes, my face pinched in pain. Gizelle's head rested in my hand. It was hard to believe I'd ever agree to stop Gizelle's sensitive heart. That didn't seem okay at all.

The vet inserted the needle with one hand and held her stethoscope to Gizelle's chest, actively listening to her heartbeat. I wanted to imagine the mastiff heartbeat sounded like a deep, noble drum. Part of me wished I could hear what the vet could hear. The sound of a heart stopping, the sound of our adventure ending. Those twelve seconds felt like an eternity. My entire adult life ran before my eyes in a series of freeze frames. The newspaper stretched across the steering wheel in Mom's Murano. Happier times with Mom, sneaking off and buying a giant puppy. The soccer goal with Fatty attached flying across the field. Our first Manhattan apartment with the sloped floor. Steaming Times Square poos. "Splish Splash, I Was Takin' a Bath" on the back patio of Rio. Walking the runway in Tompkins Square Park. Vino tasting with Conner. Dancing. Cuddling. Road trips. Running.

I watched the liquid in the tiny syringe run into Gizelle's massive body, and as it went in and her life faded out, she took some of the twenty-five-year-old me with her. The hot moisture coming out of Gizelle's nose slowed, and her head grew heavier, uninhabited by spirit, fragile in my hand. Its weight pressed my knuckles to the floor. And then it stopped. Her heart stopped.

The room went silent.

"Okay, it's done. Take your time," the vet whispered, pressing her lips into a line. She slowly moved her stethoscope into her pocket, bowed her head, and reached out to touch Gizelle one last time. I carefully slid my hand out from under Gizelle's head. I couldn't believe how immediately empty that room felt. One second her head was alive, breathing, on my hand, and the next second it wasn't. And the departure, the grand exit of her presence, was so strong and significant, it was as if she'd Tasmanian Devil-ed out of there, pouncing out of the fake living room, through the vet's office, sprinting wildly through the front doors and on to her next adventure. Her spirit's exit was so strong that when I looked back at her massive physical body on the floor, I knew Gizelle wasn't in it. *Where did she go?* I wondered. It was kind of like when you just had something in your hands, but then you set it down and you couldn't recall where you'd put it, but you knew it was there, somewhere. You knew it didn't vanish into a nothing. Gizelle didn't turn into a nothing. I felt her run away; I really did. "Please take your time." The vet repeated as she stood in the doorway. She didn't even have to say she was sorry this time. I wanted out of the room. Gizelle was not in that room anymore. So I quickly got up and left, tears running down my face again. I turned and took one last glance at her big empty body as the door closed behind me.

I hadn't exactly made a plan for my afternoon. My bus was leaving in four hours to go back to Manhattan. It was hard to be in the house, because that only reminded me of Gizelle. Caitlin and John eventually went to work. John was so heartbroken that he said he needed to do something to keep busy. Caitlin took me to get a coffee at Lil's. We sat in the window quietly together, trying to process what had happened.

Then she had to go to work, too. I was left on my own. I tried to go for a walk into downtown Portsmouth, but the cold wind was so strong it felt like it was electrocuting my face. I started walking across the World War I Memorial Bridge from Kittery to Portsmouth, and about a third of the way across I realized I couldn't do it. I didn't want to be around anyone else, or myself, for that matter, so I turned around. I needed to be in the presence of something bigger than myself, my grief. So I drove to New Castle, New Hampshire, to find the ocean.

I had driven this route with Gizelle a couple of times before. When I arrived, I saw a black-and-white lighthouse to my left, and another run-down, old brown lighthouse out in the water in front of me. The sky was blue, like Genie-from-Aladdin blue. I stood on some rocks above the beach. There were hardly waves, just the slightest ripple, and no boats or birds in sight. Everything was still. You'd think maybe I would have been done crying by now, that maybe I'd be still for a moment. But oh, no, no, no.

I howled into the ocean. A heavy cry. A cry that sounded like the hardest breathing after I had just finished running sprints on bleachers and couldn't catch my breath. I closed my eyes tightly. The subzero winds hit my face and I wondered how I had any more tears left. I held my eyes shut, and for a while I didn't breathe. I squeezed my arms around my body. I was feeling so many emotions at once: pain and anger, grief and confusion. But then I felt a sensation I cannot describe in any other way except that when I closed my eyes, I could actually see Gizelle as though she were in front of me, running. She was running as fast as she could, faster than I'd ever seen her run. She was free: her tongue flailing out of her mouth, her mouth open so wide you could see her pretty white teeth. She was in a field of purple flowers. My eyes opened to a squint and my body released its tension. I had stopped crying. I don't know when I had stopped crying, but I had. I took a breath. I could breathe.

My bus wasn't leaving to go back to Manhattan for another few hours. My rental car was packed with my things, and I wondered what to do next. The thought of another lobster roll or one more doughnut at Congdon's kind of made me want to throw up. I wasn't hungry. I wasn't thirsty. I didn't want to talk to anyone. I didn't want to write. I didn't want to do anything. How would I start my next chapter, Gizelle-less? And when I looked out into the quiet ocean, it was clear: I needed to go back to the thing I knew how to do best, the thing that came naturally to me, the only thing engrained in my body that made me feel most like myself. I got back in the car.

I drove down the coast to find a place to park. There was still dog hair in my cup holder, and I kept checking in my rearview mirror for Gizelle in the backseat. But there was no Gizelle, only evidence of our adventures in the cup holder. I kept driving. I parked in a vacant motel parking lot, threw on another pair of leggings and a jacket, and laced up my running shoes. When I got out, I was the only person in the empty parking lot. It was horribly cold, but a sunny cold. I didn't realize it then, but alone by the beach that day, I'd gotten what I'd asked for. I was traveling by myself. Totally on my own. Somewhere on the New England coast over a thousand miles away from Tennessee and three hundred miles from Manhattan. And Gizelle had brought me here. *Is this what you wanted, girl?* I thought. Looking down at my Asics, knowing exactly what she wanted.

I ran.

I ran down to the empty beach, and the cold air went straight through my double leggings and my gloves. It was so cold, it hurt. But it was a hurt that canceled out the hurt of my heart for a moment. It was like the cold wind was going to pierce my skin and rush into my ears and down into my lungs and blow away the sadness and pain. I told myself I would run a mile. A mile wasn't much. Sure, the wind stung my face, the cold air squeezed more tears from my dry eyes, and the sand slipped beneath my feet. But if I could run a mile, what else could I do?

I thought about what it takes to run the last mile of a marathon, your twenty-sixth mile, when you are really tired and you don't want to keep going. You aren't really sure if you will make it, but you keep putting one foot in front of the other, and you have to believe you can because the moment you think you can't, you won't. And once you make up your mind that you're going to do it, that you're going to keep running even though it's hard, that's when the magic happens. That's when it's almost as if some supreme backup power swoops in and says, *Here, I'm going to run this mile for you.* And next thing you know you are sprinting, you are sprinting when you never could have imagined it humanly possible to sprint, faster than you ever thought you would go. It's magic.

I felt something similar on the beach that day. Running

a mile even though it was hard. Running a mile when I was devastated. Running a mile to prove to myself that I could keep going, even when things weren't easy. And that's when magic happened. As I reached the end of my run on the empty beach that day, I looked down at my feet and there in the sand was a trail of very big paw prints.

EPILOGUE

Carry It with You

6BC Garden on East Sixth Street

After Gizelle died, Caitlin came to visit Rebecca and me in our new apartment on Avenue C in the East Village. It was the end of January—cold and dreary in Manhattan. We bundled ourselves into matching coats (never let it be said that we weren't all grateful for my time at the Gap) and walked to a cozy French restaurant called Lucien that transports you to the 7th Arrondissement for the evening. It started to snow as we walked across Fourth Street. Gentle snowflakes drifted from the winter sky and seemed to disappear just before touching the ground. They floated around us as we talked about how much we missed Gizelle, how she always looked so pretty with her brindle coat against the snow.

"It's weird," I said. "I feel her around me all the time. I feel her presence even now, walking with us." I held my arm out in the air like I was holding her leash, imagining her following us to enjoy steak frites and red wine and mussels on this cold winter night in New York City. She'd prop her head on the table and smile at us.

"I feel that, too," Caitlin added. "She's definitely around. But you know what? You know what really reminds me of Gizelle?" I took off my beanie to feel the Manhattan snow on my head, and that's when Caitlin said something I will never forget.

"You do, Lauren. You remind me of Gizelle." I smiled a teary smile. "When I'm with you, I feel like I'm with her."

I held my palm to my heart and knew that was where Gizelle lived now. Right inside of me to carry everywhere.

I was in the middle of writing this book when my mom called me from rehab on a ranch somewhere in Tennessee. "Hi, sweetie," she said. She only had seven minutes to use the phone. I could hear the ticking timer on the other line.

"Hi, Mom." I tensed a little and took a deep breath. I'd seen her maybe once in the past year and hadn't talked to her in a few months. I wondered which version of my mom was on the other line. I didn't trust her and was still struggling to make sense of her addiction, still trying to deal with the ups and downs that came with trying to have a relationship with her or trying not to have a relationship with her.

"This place is so wonderful," Mom said. "There are so many dogs here. They follow me everywhere, Fernie. I wake up at five thirty in the morning before everyone else to go for a walk on the farm, and, I'm telling you, those dogs, they wait for me! They wait by my door. I seriously just want to take one of them home. But I know I can't yet."

I let out my breath. "That's really sweet, Mommy."

"There is this one doggy named Dixie," she continued excitedly. "When you put your hand like this and you say *POW!* she turns on her back and rolls over. It's hilarious! Dixie is so smart." She got more serious. "I talk to Dixie. She listens."

I have no doubt that Dixie did listen to Mom, as she claimed. And the thought of Dixie listening to my mom, loving my mom, loving all the people in rehab, without any consideration of what their pasts held or the daily struggles they faced, was enough to make me tear up. I took another breath and focused back on our conversation. Most of our seven-minute, six-months-overdue catch-up centered on the doggies at rehab. And that was enough.

There was a time when I wanted things for my mother that she would never wish for me. *Lock her up! Punish her! Send her away forever!* I never quite realized that the only person those thoughts and resentments ever hurt was me. So I've tried taking a different approach: love Mom. I've found that letting myself love her is much easier—on everyone, including myself— than staying angry. Loving her does not mean I have to go running into her arms. Loving her means I can love her from a distance. I can remove myself. I will stay in my own lane. But I will always love her, whether she's sober or not. I'm going to trust the dogs on this one: love works best when it is given without conditions. So I'll do my best to love my mom without any. I'll try to limit my requirements of her, pray for her, let go of her, and trust that she was always doing the best she could.

What I've learned is that I am a happier person if I do not carry around the grievances I once felt about my mom. Sometimes I picture my heart like the carry-on suitcase I dream to carry around the world. There's not enough room for everything in that carry-on. So I must choose carefully, wisely. I could pack the pain I have felt in the past, especially in dealing with Mom. I could stuff all those grievances into my bag and drag them with me on my adventure—but that's a lot of weight to carry. And I certainly hope no one would carry around my shortcomings and my mistakes in their suitcase and constantly let those mistakes influence the quality of their own adventure. So I try to carry with me the things that I do love about my mom—her whimsical, childlike spirit, her positive attitude, her love for animals, her love for me. That she was the one who got me Gizelle, and Gizelle protected me. Gizelle was my best friend.

As I was writing this book, I always felt Gizelle around, at my feet or resting her nose on my computer. I miss her terribly, but whenever I do, I hold my hand to my heart and I know Gizelle is still mine to carry everywhere. And if I could carry myself like Gizelle, my big dog with the big pretty smile and even bigger heart, I will have made it. If I could find a way to live my life with her spirit and the unconditional love Gizelle showed me, I will have made it. With the ability to live in the moment, to enjoy the little things and treat every day like a fresh start, a new adventure, no matter where I am in the world or what my struggles are. Yes, to live with the unconditional love and free spirit of a dog—that would be the dream.

Acknowledgments

In an effort to keep with my theme of "lists," I made a list of people (and animals) who helped make this dream a reality. There were so many who helped me while I was writing, editing, or living this story, and I'd like to express my most sincere gratitude to all of them.

- To the dog who made this whole thing possible, my best friend, Gizelle. I always knew you would live in my heart forever, but never could I have imagined I would get to share you with others, too.
- My amazing agent, David Doerrer. Thank you for being the first person to believe in me and this story, before I even knew what it was. Thank you to Steve Ross and everyone else at Abrams.
- Karyn Marcus for editing this book and providing endless encouragement and patience. Thank you for seeing something in me and for teaching me not to use so many exclamation points.
- Christine Pride for swooping in with your expert eye and carrying us across the finish line.
- Sydney Morris for enthusiastically answering all my questions and helping me sort through thousands of Gizelle photos.

ACKNOWLEDGMENTS

- Everyone at Simon & Schuster for believing in Gizelle and taking a chance on me, especially Jonathan Karp, Richard Rhorer, Dana Trocher, and Elizabeth Gay.
- Dad for your patience and love. Thank you for always treating my dreams like they are your own and for providing a roof over my head while I wrote this. LOL.
- Tripp, you're the hardest working, funniest person I know and I love you.
- Erisy, I'm so lucky to have a little sister I look up to so much. You make me a better person.
- My sister-in-law, Jenna, who isn't an in-law at all. I don't know what I would do without you.
- My Rebecca for always listening to me and reminding me everything is okay. I think we got it right this time.
- My grandmother, Joy Hafner Bailey (aka Gandy/ Twerp), you are the reason I started writing. I love you and how and how.
- Aunt Poopers for your honesty.
- Aunt KK for being my first reader and first preorder (and for everything else).
- Aunt Laurie for being Gizelle's biggest fan.
- Aunt Lele for always helping.
- Paula for being the first person to read my first chapter.
- To the Straney Family for your support and for loving Gizelle like she was your own.
- To Katie and James (and your mastiff, Toby *G*), thank you for caring for Gizelle with such love, for finding the perfect delivery system for giving Gizelle her pills, and for being so supportive of me.
- Kimmy, thank you for the Michael Jackson dance parties in Central Park and for always riding the elevators in Times Square with me for fun. Thank you for taking care of me and Gizelle.

ACKNOWLEDGMENTS

- The Beesley Family for your help with Gizelle and our move to New York City.
- Gizelle's favorite aunts and uncles in NYC who did so much for us:

  Elan and Ashley (and Nacho, who Gizelle is very sad she never got to meet)
  Maggie, Alex, and Moxie Waffles Berman
  Danielle Owen
  Lucy Ballantyne

- Cullen Thomas, for helping that girl in your memoir class who sent you a panicky email on a Saturday morning because her story went viral and she didn't know what to do. Thank you for being the first to tell me that my story was worthy and that I could do this.
- My best high school friend, Kelley, and her brother Mitch, who lost their beautiful mother, Patti Strange, way too early. Kelley, your strength inspires me.
- Meghan and the Meehan Family.
- Lara Alammedine and Daniel Dubiecki, thank you for taking me and Gizelle under your wings and for giving me the opportunity to bring our story to the big screen.
- To Everyone at Odd Lot Entertainment, especially Rachel Shane and GiGi Pritzker.
- Andy Cochran.
- My film agent, Brad Rosenfeld, for making it happen.
- Mark Turner for his shared love of dogs.
- Norman Dwek, for sharing his home with me.
- Thank you to all of the wonderful people who wrote me or friended me or shared Gizelle's Bucket List story back in January 2015, and thank you to all of the dogs who inspired them to do so. You changed my life.

ACKNOWLEDGMENTS

- To Pamela Ann Brummet (and her beloved pup, Jackson), a thoughtful stranger and talented artist who sent me the most beautiful painting of Gizelle.
- To the English mastiff groups on Facebook, particularly the group "Drool is Cool." Writing a book about Gizelle without Gizelle was sometimes very sad, but whenever I logged onto Facebook and scrolled through our group, I found all of the mastiff love I needed. You are the best dog owners I know.
- To my new rescue dog, Bette, you are chewing on my arm right now making it difficult to type, and sometimes I swear you are part piranha, but I love you. Thank you for refilling that spot in my heart and for teaching me patience.
- Last of all, and most of all, thank you to my precious mommy. Mom, thank you for your love and generosity. I love you. I miss you. Every day I pray for you to have a good day. I hope you know how wonderful you are.
- To anyone else who struggles with addiction, I hope you find the light outside of all the chaos and lots of things to be thankful for.

About the Author

Lauren Fern Watt was born in Dallas, Texas, and grew up in the suburbs of Nashville, Tennessee. After college, she moved to a tiny New York apartment with her 160-pound English mastiff, Gizelle. Her first book, *Gizelle's Bucket List*, has been translated into fourteen languages and optioned for film. She lives in Los Angeles with her rescue dog named Bette. They continue checking things off a bucket list of their own.

To learn more about Lauren's adventures please visit:

@lfernwatt
www.laurenfornwatt.com

.